Mortgage Meltdown

Mapping the Past, Present, and Future of Fannie Mae

Julian Ashford

ISBN: 9781807650551

Published by TPSA Publishing

ENDORSEMENTS

"A writer offers an analysis of Fannie Mae's contribution to the 2008 mortgage crisis coupled with recommended reforms.

There's been no shortage of ink spilled on anatomizing the economic catastrophe of 2008, including specific analyses of the mortgage debt crisis. But there has been a surprising deficit of attention to the role played by Fannie Mae, the focus of Mukherjee's debut book. He argues that years of imprudently weak regulation led to the growth of Fannie Mae into "an unrestricted mortgage behemoth" with more than $3 trillion in assets. Fannie Mae was transformed over time—partly as a result of its winning a territorial war with the Department of Housing and Urban Development—into a government-sponsored entity with an implicit federal guarantee of its strategic bets, in effect creating an unstable model within which private reward and risk were encouraged by the promise of taxpayers' bearing the burden of failure.

At the heart of the problem was Fannie Mae's tremendously profitable guaranty arm, which allowed it to guarantee homeowner mortgages like an insurance provider in exchange for a fee. But when a deluge of home foreclosures compelled it to dole out massive payouts, Fannie Mae was egregiously short of funds since it had already spent its reserves on "doomed" bonds. The author furnishes a brief but impressively thorough history of Fannie Mae as well as an excellent primer on the housing market's basic structure.

n addition, he gives pragmatic but original solutions to the organization's troubles, starting with a reduction of liability to taxpayers by winding down its portfolio. He also advocates the creation of a private servicer enterprise, which "would have the sole purpose of servicing the 120-day delinquent mortgages" from the Government Sponsored Enterprise. Mukherjee's analysis is astonishingly concise given its breadth and, despite the technicality of the subject, remarkably accessible. He also manages to avoid even a whiff of partisan allegiance—his perspective is fashioned out of rigorous analysis versus political ideology.

Finally, his suggestions for reforming current lending practices—especially those aimed at discriminatory practices—deserve a wide audience.

An astute and wide-ranging assessment of an urgent economic problem."

—Kirkus Reviews

"This book provides an impressive overview—plus supporting details—of Fannie Mae, U.S. mortgage markets, and U.S. housing policy. It is well worth reading."

—Lawrence J. White, Professor of Economics, NYU Stern School of Business and co-author of *Guaranteed to Fail: Fannie Mae, Freddie Mac, and the Debacle of Mortgage Finance*

ACKNOWLEDGEMENTS

I wish to acknowledge the guidance provided by Professor Lawrence White at NYU Stern and Editor-in-Chief William Fitzhugh of *The Concord Review.* Their research supervision, help, and assistance were invaluable to the completion of my project.

EXECUTIVE SUMMARY

Mortgage Meltdown: Mapping the Past, Present, and Future of Fannie Mae explores the enduring relevance of Fannie Mae in the American economy, ten years after its fall in the Great Recession and eighty years after its birth in the New Deal. It charts the fatal course of Fannie Mae—as influenced by government agencies, lobbyists, congress members, and shareholders—and proposes policy for a sustainable housing future, one free from Fannie and Freddie's overhanging $100 billion liability and supportive of America's commitment to homeownership.

The book begins with a contextualization of Fannie Mae's functionality within the mortgage market, providing an in-depth look at the business model and interactions between the primary and secondary mortgage markets as a fictitious newlywed couple, the Smiths, take out a mortgage. It then proceeds with Fannie's history, beginning with its 1938 humble birth in President Roosevelt's New Deal as the "Federal National Mortgage Association." The organization grew steadily but silently until the mid-1950s, cementing the Uncle Sam's role in American mortgage policy. But as Vietnam War costs brought concerns about government debt, President Johnson realized he could swiftly avoid an additional $2.5 billion budgetary burden by privatizing Fannie. So he did, resulting in a shareholder-owned Fannie Mae with an "implicit" government guarantee.

Following the completed privatization in 1970, the Department of Housing and Urban Development (HUD) became Fannie Mae's new regulator. The relationship proved to be problematic as conflicting housing policy ideologies—one to support lower-income housing and one to support profitability—morphed into an ambitious endeavor to support homeownership while chasing billions in profits. Between the mid-1980s to 2000s, Fannie Mae announced a trillion-dollar commitment to support lower-income housing and reported billions in annual profit, all while developing new securities in the mortgage market: mortgage-backed securities (MBS). Yet the rise of new competition, private-label mortgages, and securitization led to a slippery slope of moral ambiguities and subprime lending. This book posits that Fannie Mae, private-label mortgage providers, banks, rating companies, and government agencies were collectively negligent for the buildup to the financial crisis. When the unsustainable solution collapsed, Fannie and Freddie received the costliest bailout in history—$188 billion dollars.

Mortgage Meltdown then begins translating Fannie Mae's past by exploring and analyzing notable reform measures (Corker-Warner, Johnson-Crapo, New York Federal Reserve, and Risk Sharing) before proposing unique policy recommendations. The premises of reform are (a) reducing Fannie's outstanding liability on taxpayers while (b) maintaining a commitment to American homeownership.

Mortgage Meltdown features a two-fold process to reduce Fannie's liability: winding down its role in the housing market and introducing private enterprises. The proposal attempts to reduce the toll of home foreclosure, a catalyst in draining Fannie's funds during the Great Recession, on the institutions involved in the mortgage market, by encouraging the creation of independent but prudently regulated Private Servicer Enterprises (PSEs) to reduce the systemic risk in the mortgage market. The PSEs would only intervene when Fannie is obligated to act upon its guaranty commitment (the 120th-day) to facilitate a joint payment between the struggling homeowner and Fannie Mae. Benefits to this system include a deferring of the immediate capital drain caused by Fannie's guaranty business and an alternative pathway for the homeowner to avoid foreclosure. PSE functions, operations, incentives, and regulations are also detailed.

The book also suggests sustaining American homeownership through measures relying less on mortgage finance and increasingly on supply-side reforms. It addresses the nation's relative historical low of 64% homeownership (far below the 68–69% in the mid-2000s) and the aging, waning housing stock by encouraging the overhaul and expansion of the Community Reinvestment Act and local suburban neighborhood building codes and the implementation of stricter federal penalties against discriminatory lending. Eliminating mortgage lending discrimination and providing greater housing and mortgage access should be priorities in supporting a sustainable future for American homeownership.

TABLE OF CONTENTS

INTRODUCTION

The Federal National Mortgage Association (FNMA) was not heralded with much attention when chartered by President Franklin D. Roosevelt on February 10, 1938.[1] Notable press coverage included just an eight-sentence article in *The Wall Street Journal*. Yet eighty years later, the FNMA ("Fannie Mae") is consistently featured in the headlines of international newspapers. An organization that had humble beginnings in the New Deal, crafted as a "provisional response" to the Great Depression, has transformed into a cornerstone of the American housing market. Considering that the housing sector comprises 15.3% of the nation's $19 trillion GDP, Fannie Mae has become an essential component of our overall present-day economy as well.[2]

Mortgage Meltdown: Mapping the Past, Present, and Future of Fannie Mae begins by exploring Fannie's history. The book traces the themes of conflicting housing policy ideologies and subdued business model regulations to demonstrate how specific shortcomings in housing legislation led to an unrestricted mortgage behemoth—one with $3.25 trillion in assets.[3] Next, it proposes policy for a sustainable mortgage future, one free from Fannie and Freddie's overhanging $100 billion liability and supportive of America's commitment to homeownership.

The first chapter, "The Secret Lives of Residential Mortgages," contextualizes the remainder of the book by providing a guidebook on Fannie Mae's functionality in the mortgage market while defining and clarifying relevant mortgage terms and concepts. Next, "Inception" explores Fannie's creation, highlighting the significance of the 1920s credit system, examining President Roosevelt's response to the 1933 mortgage crisis, and defining Fannie's early business model. The following chapter, "Privatization," details Fannie Mae's intricate relationship with the government and analyzes President Johnson's cumbersome privatization attempt. "Politics and Profits" then deconstructs Fannie's rivalry with the Department of Housing and Urban Development (HUD), outlining how Fannie's perpetual public-private conflict disadvantaged millions of Americans. The "Faltering Business Model" chapter describes the flawed changes to Fannie's business structure, largely as a result of stricter yet ineffective regulation. Together, "Politics and Profits" and "Faltering Business Model" track the seeds of conflict into the early 2000s, leading up to the "The Crisis." This chapter begins by exploring Fannie's new private competition and concludes by examining Fannie's involvement in the crisis under the premises of counterproductive housing policy and unchecked business model growth, demonstrating how Fannie's demise can be traced to a few critical moments. After analyzing Fannie Mae's past, the book briefly examines notable reform measures in "Proposal Review" before suggesting new policies in "Recommendations." The premises of reform are (a) reducing Fannie's liability on taxpayers through winding down Fannie's role and creating private enterprises while (b) supporting American homeownership by restricting discriminatory lending practices and improving mortgage and housing availability.

The difficulty lies, not in the new ideas, but in escaping from the old ones.

—Keynes, The General Theory of Employment, Interest, and Money[4]

1. THE SECRET LIVES OF RESIDENTIAL MORTGAGES

1.1. The Primary Mortgage Market

Most adult Americans, about 65%, have purchased a home in their lifetime, and almost 90% of homebuyers in the United States take out a home mortgage.[5] Totaling nearly $10 trillion, residential mortgage loans finance over 50 million households and are the second-largest US debt issued, behind only US Treasury bonds.[6] By tracing the path of a residential mortgage through the financial realm, we can better understand Fannie Mae's function and composition.

Suppose Mr. and Mrs. Smith are buying a home. They've got their eyes on a beautiful home in Massachusetts, a classic English colonial. Bright light, large walk-in-closets, and a recently renovated kitchen seal the deal for the Smiths. The price comes in at a hefty $500,000, but the Smiths are tired of renting. They readily accept and get their paperwork ready for a mortgage, a large loan taken to buy a home.

The Smiths consult a mortgage originator, a lending institution that will help them complete their home transaction. Among many others, companies in the origination business include Wells Fargo, Bank of America, and Quicken Loans. The Smiths choose a local Wells Fargo branch, where bank representatives perform a thorough check on the Smiths' financials, including lending history, employment history, FICO credit score, assets, and annual income. Before loaning to the Smiths, Wells Fargo must ensure that clients have a relatively low chance of defaulting[7] on mortgage payments. With homes generally being the costliest purchases most Americans make, Wells Fargo has a significant amount of money at stake when originating mortgages. Therefore, prospective homebuyers are classified as either "prime" or "subprime"[8] borrowers. "Prime" indicates a relatively low risk of default; loaning to this type of borrower is a safe, reliable play for the originator. However, "subprime" connotes higher risk in lending; buyers classified as subprime lack sustainable incomes and healthy credit (usually a FICO score < 635).[9] Both Mr. and Mrs. Smith have good credit scores and incomes and are given a "prime" rating, meaning that Wells Fargo can confidently give them a mortgage.

The Smiths then negotiate the terms of their mortgage contract. All mortgage contracts have four crucial elements: (a) principal, the value of the money loaned; (b) interest, the mortgage rate of borrowing the principal and the originator's incentive to lend; (c) taxes, the state and local property taxes on the transaction; and (d) insurance, the safeguard against theft, natural disasters, and other hazards. Traditionally, mortgage principals are approximately 80% of the home value (in the Smiths' case, the loan principal would be $500,000 x .80 = $400,000). Taxes and insurance are generally held in escrow[10] to preempt homeowner defaults on tax obligations and mitigate potential risk for insurance agencies. Although the mortgage rate can either remain fixed (fixed-rate mortgage) or adjustable (adjustable-rate mortgage), individual lenders have specific mortgage rates and incentives. The Smiths also choose the duration of their mortgage contract, surveying the popular 10-year, 15-year, 20-year, and 30-year options. Currently, about 80% of American mortgages are held in a 30-year term length.[11]

A month or two after the Smiths finalize their application with the local Wells Fargo branch, they secure their mortgage. Upon receiving approval for their loan principal, contract duration, and mortgage rate, the Smiths continue on to buying their dream home. They'll pay their mortgage each month, hopefully enjoying their home as well. For the Smiths, their mortgage experience ends with either the monthly mortgage payment or a "mortgage prepayment," a term that describes a lump-sum loan repayment before the contract termination date. Meanwhile, the originator profits from the interest rate on the mortgage, which varies between contracts but currently hovers around 4% for a standard 30-year loan.[12] During the life of a mortgage loan, the loaned balance is amortized, or reduced, until completely paid off. The borrower usually repays the loan (both the principal and interest) through the "level payment" structure, a standard of mortgages that requires the same payment amount each month.

Yet the Smiths may not even be sending their mortgage payments or prepayment directly to their lender, the local Wells Fargo branch. Instead, mortgage payments are usually addressed to a mortgage servicer, an institution that collects monthly payments, sends payment notices and reminders to borrowers, maintains records of principal balances, and even initiates foreclosure when appropriate.[13] Essentially, mortgage servicers receive and forward the proceeds of a monthly mortgage payment to the investors, profiting from servicing fees for their work. Mortgage servicers, like SunTrust Mortgage and Wells Fargo Servicing, ensure that the lender receives the payment but follow up on the direct interactions with borrowers. Sometimes, as in the case of Wells Fargo, the originator and servicer are different arms of the same institution.

The situation described above (the Smiths' buying quest, the mortgage originator, and the mortgage servicer) is all encompassed by one term: the primary mortgage market. This market involves direct interactions with homebuyers and homeowners. However, the monthly mortgage payment from the Smiths does not rest solely with the originator; the Smiths' mortgage money travels well beyond the primary mortgage market.

1.2. The Secondary Mortgage Market

Enter the secondary mortgage market: the second and lesser-known section of the mortgage spectrum. In addition to engaging with the Smiths, the local Wells Fargo branch also interacts with hundreds of other homebuyers. Likewise, Wells Fargo as a national bank makes millions of mortgage originations each year, currently having $450 billion worth of mortgage loans in its portfolio.[14] These millions of mortgage loans, given to millions of different borrowers, provide an excellent investment opportunity for mortgage originators.

Although the ultimate objective of originators is to trade their mortgage loans in the secondary mortgage market, they must follow a sequence of steps to initiate loans for trading. First, Wells Fargo will group its mortgages together through "pooling," a process that involves organizing mortgages into similar bundles based on borrower characteristics (FICO score, loan principal, prime vs. subprime). Next, Wells Fargo will create bonds from these pooled mortgages, known as mortgage-backed securities bonds (MBS bonds). Wells Fargo will then be able to sell its residential mortgage loans—in the form of MBS bonds—within the trading network of the secondary mortgage market. These securities[15] are traded in a market between mortgage lenders, broker-dealers, hedge funds, banks, the Federal Reserve, and even Fannie Mae and Freddie Mac. The Federal Reserve, for example, stepped in and bought mortgage pools during Quantitative Easing efforts when it attempted to stimulate the economy.

The secondary market is an efficient mechanism to maintain lender liquidity, considering the potentially restrictive long-term nature of mortgage loans. Selling MBS bonds supplies mortgage lenders with infusions of capital to continue making home loans while providing a profitable investment opportunity for banks, funds, and other financial institutions. Before the secondary market was established in the 1980s, only larger banks could hold out for the duration of a 15- to 30-year loan, leading to lower credit availability for new homebuyers. Once introduced, the secondary market contributed to the rise in American homeownership rates, from about 64% in 1985 to a peak of almost 68% in 2006.[16] Historically, banks hold about 23% of the MBS market, even more than their 17% share in the US Treasury portfolio.[17] The secondary mortgage market (Fig 1.1) has grown exponentially since its introduction in the 1980s and is now worth over $6 trillion.[18]

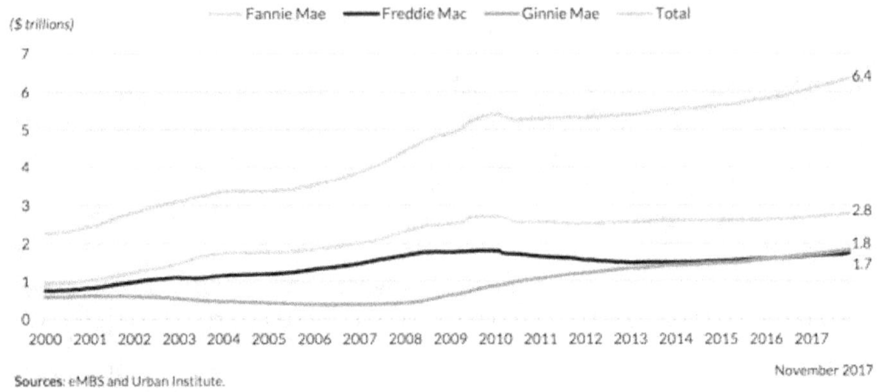

Figure 1.1: Secondary Mortgage Market Growth *(Source: Urban Institute)*

Aside from alleviating illiquidity among mortgage originators, the MBS market remains a profitable investment for many investors enticed by the relatively low levels of risk. Fannie Mae and Freddie Mac, the cornerstones of the secondary mortgage market, ensure just that: low risk. When lenders like Wells Fargo pool mortgages to sell MBS bonds, investors are initially skeptical about investment risk because MBS bonds do not guarantee any favorable return. Wells Fargo has maintained relatively stable financial health, despite its 2018 scandal and worsening reputation, so the chance of failure and loss can persist in investors' minds. But if Wells Fargo turns to Fannie Mae, then investors' worries are put to ease.

Fannie Mae, a nickname for the Federal National Mortgage Association, will guarantee Wells Fargo's (and all other mortgage lenders') MBSs from potential loss. Wells Fargo approaches Fannie with pools of mortgages, which Fannie restructures into mortgage-backed securities. If homeowners like the Smiths default or foreclose, Fannie will cover the losses for the investors of the MBS, eliminating any chance of loss. Fannie Mae's controversial government guarantee, which is explored in later sections, allows it to stomach the potential losses from foreclosure. In the case of homeowner default, Fannie will pay the entire loan in a lump-sum payment to investors, effectively removing the chance of loss and incentivizing investment in MBS bonds. However, for its services, Fannie charges a guaranty fee (g-fee): Fannie is compensated through homeowner's mortgage interest rate. For example, if the Smiths' mortgage rate is 4.25%, and Fannie charges its standard 0.57% g-fee, the remaining 3.68% is shared between the mortgage servicer (which has a fee varying from 0.25% to 0.5%) and the MBS bond investors.[19] Essentially, Fannie's guaranty process involves purchasing pools of mortgages from the lenders, securitizing them, and selling them as "Fannie Mae MBSs" in the secondary mortgage market.

Fannie's guaranty process is a routine procedure. First, Fannie must securitize the mortgage pools in accordance with the MBS Trust rules and restrictions. The MBS Trust guidelines offer specific instructions for MBS issuance, pooling requirements, and investor payment structure. Upon proper creation of the MBS, Fannie recruits a mortgage servicer to follow through with the receiving and distributing of the MBS bond proceeds. Last, depending on whether Fannie owns the MBS itself, Fannie either sells the MBS bonds directly to investors or gives them back to the lender for trading.

Ultimately, when the Smiths pay their monthly mortgage, money from their payment is not restricted to the primary mortgage market. Some remains with the mortgage servicer as a service fee and some with Fannie Mae for the guaranty fee, but the majority rests with the investors—the broker-dealers, banks, and funds that invested in the MBS bonds. As the secondary mortgage market became an integral section of the broader financial market over the past thirty years, Fannie Mae has quietly amassed undeniable importance.[20]

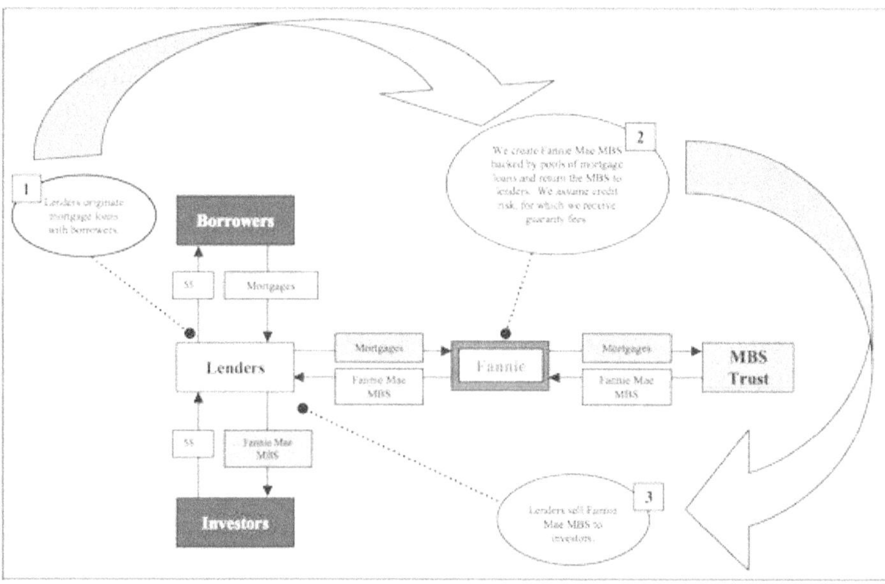

Figure 1.2: Mortgage Market Flowchart *(Source: Fannie Mae)*

1.3. Foreclosures

When a homeowner misses a monthly mortgage payment, he or she faces a "mortgage delinquency"; whether the payment is missed by three days or three weeks, the homeowner can still make the mortgage payment. Although specific policy varies between states, the delinquency process formally begins when the homeowner becomes 30 days or 60 days delinquent.[21] Mortgage companies recognize that homeowners might be facing short-term financial crunches, and servicers attempt frequent contact with homeowners for the first three to six months. If calls are ignored, however, the foreclosure process begins much faster.

Once the servicer has sufficient reason to believe the homeowner is unable to pay (in a state of "mortgage default"), the company files a public Notice of Default, known as a *lis pendens*.[22] Three types of foreclosure can be initiated at this point: strict foreclosure, judicial foreclosure, or statutory foreclosures. A "foreclosure" is an attempt by the mortgage lender to recover the value of the remaining mortgage loan balance from a homeowner through the action of taking possession of the property. Strict foreclosure involves a lender lawsuit to indicate a specific time frame for borrower payment. If the borrower is unable to pay, the mortgage holder directly seizes the property. A judicial foreclosure necessitates a similar lawsuit filed through the justice system, but the borrower has only 30 days to make a payment. Additionally, the property is sold through an auction conducted by the court to the highest bidder, allowing the lender to recover the loss. Last, a statutory foreclosure is applicable only if the original contract contains a "power of sale" clause.[23] After the default notices are sent and the waiting period passes, the mortgage company itself carries out an auction to recuperate the loss. A homeowner can, however, avoid a foreclosure through multiple actions, including catching up on missed mortgage payments or inducing a short sale—selling the property for less than the loan value.

From the perspective of the secondary mortgage market, a foreclosure entails Fannie Mae acting on its guaranty to cover the losses in case of homeowner default. At the 120-day delinquent status, the mortgage will be removed from the MBS bond and instead placed into Fannie's internal portfolio. Through an up-front lump-sum payment, Fannie will reimburse the remaining principal on the mortgage to the MBS investors. The system works smoothly in favorable economic times, but the rampant foreclosures can be swift and deadly. Between mid-2007 and 2017, more than 7.5 million homes were foreclosed, but the foreclosure rate—the share of all home loans in foreclosure—fell from a peak of 3.6% in 2011 to 0.9% in December 2016.[24] Waves of foreclosures caused tremendous stress in both the mortgage market and the financial system. For Wall Street, Bear Stearns's disclosure of two failed subprime-orientated hedge funds initiated a string of bankruptcies. For Fannie and

Freddie, the government was forced to intervene with a $187.5 billion bailout.[25]

The Smiths and their mortgage loan exemplify the interconnectedness of the primary and secondary markets, but home foreclosure warns of their potentially dangerous nature. Fannie Mae is the backbone of the secondary mortgage market, allowing a system of MBS trading to thrive between various financial institutions and organizations. A backbone is essential in human movement and activity, as is the mortgage market in the American economy. Fannie Mae supports everything, just like the backbone, but millions of Americans exactly like the Smiths are the real roots of the entire mortgage market.

Fannie Mae was created to serve the American Dream of homeownership.

—Bethany McLean, Shaky Ground: The Strange Saga of the U.S. Mortgage Giants[26]

2. INCEPTION

2.1. The Rise of the Credit System

The Roaring Twenties were characterized by laissez-faire economic policy that, leading to a period of sustained economic prosperity, caused significant changes in American lifestyle and culture. Americans splurged on new products like automobiles and radios, enjoyed an era of new fashion and dance, and ignited movements of progressivism. The 1920s also marked the beginning of the American consumer economy. Average annual earnings nearly doubled from $708 in 1916 to $1303 in 1924, and the additional disposable income led to luxuries becoming staples in many American households.[27] Moreover, the introduction of buying on credit directly translated into exponential increases in consumer spending.

The single greatest source of risk for the credit system, however, became the rapidly expanding residential housing sector. Home mortgages were readily offered through commercial banks, mutual savings banks, and thrifts, resulting in American consumer debt more than doubling between 1920 and 1930.[28] The credit system marked the beginning of a shift in traditional American thinking. Homeownership became a national priority and a quantifier of the American Dream for the fledging middle class. The housing boom of the 1920s added 2.6 million units, approximately double the annual magnitude of the 2000s boom (1.3 million units).[29] Banks capitalized on the growing demand, keeping mortgage rates stable at 6.1% throughout the decade. As consumers developed an iron stomach for credit, politicians warmed to regulatory policy that allowed for more debt.

2.2. Roosevelt's Response

Soon, the Black Tuesday stock market crash, coupled with the ill-thought regulation policies and the overwhelming credit situation, led to a financial panic. The Great Depression persists as one of America's weakest moments, with widespread poverty, unemployment rates in the mid-20% range, and a psychological scarring. With a shortage of money due to "hoarding" and waning investor activity, the banking sector collapsed.[30]

In 1932, President Franklin D. Roosevelt was elected on the premises of economic empowerment, and he spent his first hundred days dedicated to his Alphabet Agencies. Though his New Deal is most iconic for agencies like the Works Progress Administration and Civilian Conservation Corps, Roosevelt also addressed the impending housing crisis in his economic revival agenda. The ripples of unemployment and consumer debt had quickly escalated into a national mortgage crisis: about 50% of all mortgage debt was predicted to default by 1933.[31] The materialistic culture of the Roaring Twenties had fueled demand for newer and larger homes, but in the aftermath of Black Tuesday, the housing industry struggled as national home construction projects hovered around 93,000, only 10% of their 1920s peak.[32]

Fortunately for both Roosevelt and Congress, rising unemployment and the housing slump were closely intertwined; about one in three unemployed Americans had previously held a construction occupation.[33] Roosevelt's plan, then, was to get people back to work by building houses. With a revived housing industry and reduced unemployment, stress could be relieved from the banking industry and the overall economy. However, lending to homebuyers and homebuilders required significant funding, so Roosevelt needed the support of the banks to fulfill his plan. Yet almost half of the nation's banks, approximately 11,000 out of the total 25,000, had failed since Black Tuesday, and the ones remaining did not want to take any risks.[34] Thus, Roosevelt's new mission became to provide confidence to the banks so they would lend money to finance homes. In the Housing Act of 1934, the Federal Housing Administration (FHA) was drafted as an insurance provider to mortgage-supplying banks.[35] With an insurance service to reduce the loss associated with mortgage default, Roosevelt hoped the minute insurance costs in exchange for safeguarding against massive mortgage risk would prompt more lending.

Although lending volume did increase, the banks did not have enough capital to make a notable impact on the housing industry to jump-start the economy. Consequently, a new idea emerged: the government would create a mortgage association that would buy and sell mortgages insured by the FHA (FHA-insured mortgages). This association, using money from private investors, would replenish the banks' dry capital so more loans could be made. Unfortunately, no association like this was ever formed, as private investors were "so pessimistic that no one would put up money for the common good."[36] Thus, Roosevelt decided to have a government agency buy the FHA-insured mortgages. On February 10, 1938, a special branch of the existing Reconstruction Finance Corporation was repurposed into buying FHA-insured mortgages, and the Federal National Mortgage Association (FNMA) was born.[37]

2.3. The FNMA's Original Purpose

The FNMA would borrow from the US Treasury to buy FHA-insured mortgages from commercial banks. By selling the money-draining mortgage loans off their balance sheets, the banks would subsequently have a steady stream of money, with which more mortgages could be granted and ultimately more homes bought and sold. The FNMA was *not* a profit-driven organization; its primary purpose was to stimulate the housing market by purchasing, holding, and selling FHA-insured loans as it saw necessary. In its first year, the FNMA bought 26,276 mortgages, a relatively small amount considering America's population of nearly 135 million people, and saw only 25 foreclosures. Additionally, the provisions for the strict $220 million borrowing limit and purchasing cap-off in the FNMA's charter strongly suggested that Roosevelt had sought only a provisional response to the housing crisis.[38] Considering the initial attempt to encourage private mortgage associations in 1934 before settling for the creation of a government agency in 1938, Roosevelt's actions conveyed his ultimate vision for a shareholder-owned solution to the mortgage market.

Although the extent of the FNMA's interaction was intended to be limited to commercial banks, the FNMA began influencing American homeownership policy. Within five years, banks that sold FHA-insured mortgages offered incentives to attract more homebuyers. In 1935 mortgage rates held at 5.5% and contract lengths at 10 years, but in 1943 mortgage rates fell below 5%, and contract lengths averaged 15 years, a realization of Roosevelt's efforts and banks' growing willingness to lend.[39] Lower-income homebuyers flocked to these banks—particularly thrifts—and thus the FNMA served as a governmental mechanism to help thousands of displaced Americans find housing and was ultimately a precursor of future attempts to cultivate lower-income housing programs. The creation of the FNMA would cement the government's role in American housing policy; it would be seen as an agency dedicated to helping underserved Americans achieve their "American Dream" of homeownership.

These [government-chartered corporations], though they may have been useful for the first introduction, have in the long run proved, universally, either burdensome or useless.

—Smith, An Inquiry into the Nature and Causes of the Wealth of Nations[40]

3. PRIVATIZATION

3.1. Rechartering the FNMA

When World War II drew to a close in 1945, Americans rejoiced at the defeats of Germany and Japan but held a wary watch on the Soviet Union. US foreign policy officials worked strenuously to prevent another global conflict, and domestic war-related policy focused on addressing veterans' needs, including education, medicine, and housing. As approximately 10 million troops demobilized, the Truman administration sought to ensure veterans access to new homes, and President Harry S. Truman allowed the Veterans Administration to guarantee home loans for veterans. Eventually, in the Housing Act of 1949, Truman gave the FNMA permission to purchase Veterans Administration–insured mortgages. With the influx of veteran home purchases, the FNMA's portfolio steadily grew from a mere $210 million in 1942 to an astronomical $2.5 billion only a decade later.[41] As the FNMA's initial borrowing limits and financial restrictions were hastily adjusted, critics accused the FNMA of "bursting out of its confines." Accompanying the exponential growth of the FNMA's portfolio came a notable accumulation of debt; as the majority of the FNMA's mortgage purchases were financed by debt holdings, its debt soon ballooned to over $2 billion.[42]

In 1953, President Dwight D. Eisenhower stepped into the White House. Eisenhower credited himself with dismantling several of FDR's New Deal programs, and his attitude toward the FNMA was no different. Concerned with the government's over-involvement in housing, Eisenhower sought advice from many economists and government officials. Miles Colean, a mortgage consultant, shared Eisenhower's views, writing to the president that "the federal policy [toward housing] should be one of aiding to stabilize the flow of private funds. It should not be one of exercising direct and detailed influence on the building market or of entering the lending market directly, or indirectly, with government funds."[43]

Soon, Eisenhower drafted legislation to get the government out of mortgages. The 1954 Charter Act aimed to recharter Fannie Mae as a corporation with "mixed" ownership. In his law, Eisenhower tried to break the FNMA into three distinct sections. Two branches would be part of the government: one accountable for "special assistance" in serving the public interest and the second responsible for the liquidation of all mortgages acquired before 1954. The third section would be independent of the government, but it would seek to do the same job that the FNMA previously did.[44] Eventually, the goal was to have a completely private company handling all of the FNMA's affairs. Although Eisenhower's 1954 Charter Act passed, and his break-up plan was economically sound, his law was largely ignored. Since there was no deadline or any sort of legal mechanism to ensure the law was enforced, it was largely disregarded, and the FNMA continued to operate as a government entity. The burden of dealing with the FNMA fell on another president.

3.2. Modifying the FNMA

Whereas World War II and the millions of demobilized American troops buying homes had given the FNMA an opportunity to rapidly grow and expand, turning a $4.4 million portfolio in 1947 into one worth more than $2.5 billion in 1953, the Vietnam War would have a different consequence.[45] When Lyndon B. Johnson took the White House in 1963, he faced severe economic challenges, most notably rising debt levels. In 1966, as Johnson fought with Congress over grueling war costs, he created the President's Commission of Budget Concepts, tasked with improving budgetary accounting methods. In its study, the commission recommended that the debts of government agencies, like the FNMA, be included in the federal budget. The FNMA's debt would alone add $2.5 billion, roughly 60% of the current national deficit.[46]

Johnson swiftly decided to reduce government involvement from the mortgage sector and repurpose the FNMA as a private, shareholder-owned entity. To aid in the transition process, he established a mortgage task force of representatives from the Bureau of the Budget, the Treasury and Federal Reserve Boards, and the Department of Housing and Urban Development (HUD) to analyze Eisenhower's forgotten legislation and make new recommendations for housing finance reform.[47] While each institution had its own intentions and priorities, the task force's recommendation would also have to please the American homebuilders and Realtors, dominant components of the home-construction industry. Although the perspectives of different institutions could have given the collaboration extra depth, a conflict of interest led to a power struggle between private interests and public-policy goals.

The view that private shareholders, primarily interested in profits over mandated policy, favored relatively weak government involvement would be an oversimplification of the debate. On the contrary, the officials supporting a weaker FNMA had little shared interest. The shareholder perspective in the new FNMA supported the views of Realtors, homebuilders, and housing-sector veterans interested in financial sustainability, and the Johnson Administration and Bureau of the Budget representatives also favored weak government participation. Johnson needed to manage more pressing issues regarding the national debt and had intended only a write-off of the FNMA's debts: he had little desire to modify the FNMA beyond removing the liability for his taxpayers (voters). Meanwhile, homebuilders and Realtors favored a weak FNMA that would allow them greater autonomy in the housing sector, and Realtors especially favored a mortgage association independent of the HUD. Such an organization, they feared, would only lead to government partiality and preference for Realtors representing urban communities.

The HUD, however, strongly favored close regulation over the FNMA, to the extent that HUD Secretary Robert Weaver proclaimed that the FNMA should be "completely staffed and operated by government and completely under government control."[48] Understandably, the reasoning behind the HUD's desires stemmed from the fear that the privately established FNMA would betray urban housing policy initiatives, rendering a government mechanism unable to achieve its original purpose. The FNMA had been a useful tool in aiding Americans thus far, helping not only thousands of veterans but also thousands of economically disadvantaged Americans living in urban communities. Yet beyond doubts of the FNMA's reliability to promote housing initiatives, the HUD had a stronger personal stake in the matter: with the passing of the landmark Fair Housing Act of 1968 a few months prior, the HUD had thought of itself as an invincible government agency that could promote both social good and economic sustainability. The HUD adamantly refused to back down until the Bureau of the Budget threatened budgetary cuts. Ultimately, a compromise between the components of the mortgage task force led to the passing and signing of the Housing and Urban Development Act in 1968.

3.3. Advantage Fannie Mae

On May 21, 1970, the new FNMA—now referred to as Fannie Mae—transitioned into a shareholder-owned company.[49] Fannie Mae's board was composed of fifteen members: five chosen by the White House and ten chosen by shareholders. The privatized Fannie enjoyed numerous economic benefits over its few competitors. To begin, Fannie was exempt from state income taxes and Securities and Exchange Commission (SEC) fees, allowing for greater net profits in decades to come.[50] Fannie enjoyed low borrowing rates, essential in its pursuit to profit from buying mortgage pools. Next, Fannie faced few regulatory requirements—it was exempt from SEC disclosure and financial-reporting regulations, a measure that would severely inhibit transparency into the financial accounts of the organization.

Most importantly, Fannie had an "implicit" government guarantee. Although no mention of a government bailout was "explicitly" added to Fannie's charter, two key indications denote Fannie's "special status." First, commercial banks had no limit to the funds they could invest in Fannie Mae bonds, suggesting Fannie would be considered virtually as safe as benchmark US Treasury bonds. Second, the government could buy 90% of Fannie's debt ($2.25 billion out of $2.5 billion at the time) if Fannie ever needed financial support.[51] Fannie's debt would grow in the coming years, maturing to nearly $1.75 trillion in 2008,[52] but the debt-purchasing clause would not be adjusted; the government would continue to issue verbal agreements. Fannie's comprehensive restructuring had little economic significance for the American public. Ideologically, however, investors came to view Fannie as another arm of Uncle Sam. If anything bad were to happen, he would surely be there to help out. Inaugural Fannie Mae president Raymond Lapin prophesied on the state of the "weird hybrid," a challenge Fannie endures today:

The new private corporation must remain publicly oriented despite its private ownership.

—Raymond Lapin, President of Fannie Mae, 1967–1969[53]

4. POLITICS AND PROFITS

4.1. HUD Chronicles

Fundamentally, Fannie Mae had been made independent of the government in order to avoid a budgetary burden. But with the advantages of government sponsorship, the road was paved for Fannie to dominate the mortgage market. President Johnson did not foresee a contradiction between private profits and public interest notes Joseph Califano Jr., his personal assistant. President Johnson believed the new Fannie would "leverage federal power": Fannie Mae would promote the overall housing market without adding to America's debt.[54] Reflective of this view, Johnson's legislation largely dodged the controversial question of government involvement with relatively ambiguous language. Fannie's charter included provisions to "provide supplemental assistance for...residential mortgages (including activities relating to mortgages on housing for low-income families...involving a reasonable economic return)."[55] The extent of the "supplemental assistance" was to be determined periodically upon extensive study by federal regulators, and the "reasonable economic return" remained undefined. Examining the charter reveals a cloud of vagueness surrounding the HUD's involvement in Fannie Mae's future, and Johnson's inability to foresee or resolve the public/private debate would catalyze future Fannie policy. For the next two decades, as Fannie's profits steadily rose, the HUD never reduced pressures to support the low-income spectrum. When President George H. W. Bush signed the Federal Housing Enterprises Financial Safety and Soundness Act (FHEFSSA) in 1992, officials thought Fannie could be reeled in, but FHEFSSA, too, had multiple stumbling blocks.

FHEFSSA established the HUD as Fannie's mission regulator: the HUD would look into whether or not Fannie reached out to support low-income housing and underserved areas. Fannie's direct regulator, the Office of Federal Housing Enterprise Oversight (OFHEO), was weak and underfunded.[56] Every year, Congress delayed approval on OFHEO's budget, leaving the agency constantly unsure about hiring. OFHEO director Armando Falcon noted that he had only twenty regulators, while a standard federal bank regulator dealing with similar risk could allocate sixty examiners, suggesting Congress had responded a Fannie Mar $200 million lobbying package.[57]

Meanwhile, the HUD continued to pressure Fannie's purchasing agenda. To start, Fannie was expected to devote 30% of mortgage purchases to serve low-income groups.[58] Congress realized that low-income groups had higher chances of foreclosures, so the FHEFSSA included provisions to define a "conforming loan," a loan deemed safe enough for Fannie to purchase. In 1992, Fannie Mae's pursuance of mortgages was capped at loan values exceeding $202,300.[59] Additional guidelines were loose as well as loosely maintained, with no specific FICO score requirements or other identity or pay verifications. The extent of pursuable risk was not clear, and that served to the advantage of Fannie.

By 1995 Fannie began taking on riskier assets, coupling the HUD's reinvigorated push to support lower-income housing with the ambiguity in "conforming loans." Fannie began guaranteeing mortgages from borrowers who had lower FICO credit scores and higher mortgage loan-to-value ratios (LTVs).[60] In 1992 16% of Fannie's holdings had LTVs greater than the standard of 80%. In 1993 it became 19%, and by the late 1990s, a quarter of Fannie's holdings had LTVs greater than 80%.[61] Fannie Mae began pushing into the higher-risk market, partially on direct instruction from the HUD and FHEFSSA. Indeed, Fannie was helping mortgages flow to economically disadvantaged Americans, but its practices were on a soon-to-be fatal course.

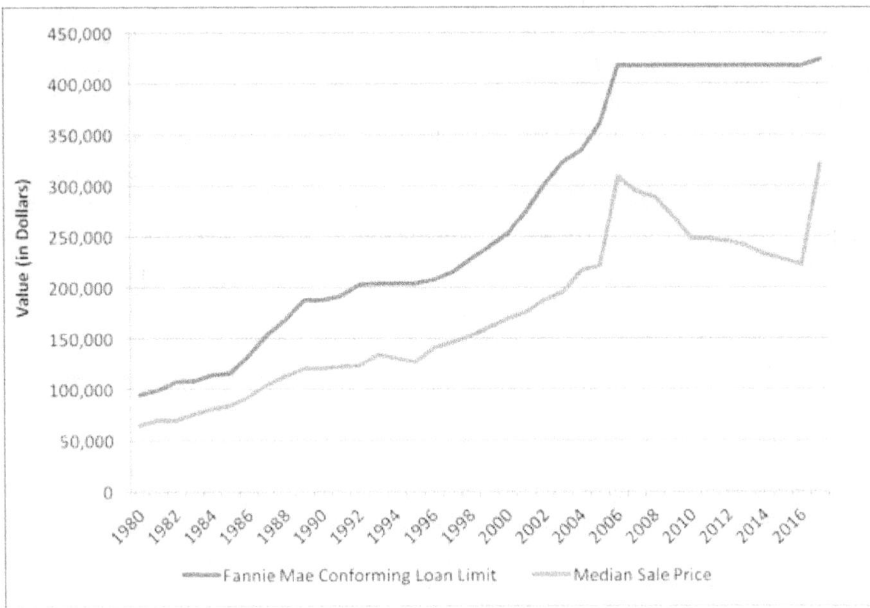

Figure 4.1: Historical Fannie Mae Loan Limit and Median Sale Price *(Source: Fannie Mae and US Census)*

With a wider net of mortgages to purchase and profit from, Fannie Mae's net income kept rising in the late 1990s. Fannie's profit rose from $3.4 billion in 1998 to $4.4 billion in 2000.[62] As Fannie became more profitable, HUD Secretary Andrew Cuomo pressured it to prove its public purpose. In 1999 he recommended Fannie devote half of its business toward lower-income housing. Cuomo had calculated that the new regulations would provide housing to an additional 28 million Americans within a couple of years, theoretically without spending a federal penny.[63] Pushed by Cuomo and the HUD, Fannie Mae increased mortgage purchases dramatically. In 1998 Fannie's mortgage portfolio totaled $415 billion, but in 2003, that number had almost tripled, reaching more than $1 trillion.[64]

Fannie Mae's privatization in 1968 and FHEFSSA's in 1992 compounded the ideological conflict between Fannie's shareholder interests and the HUD's policy missions. From the birth of a "weird hybrid" came a Fannie Mae that was developing an appetite for risk unchecked by sound regulation.[65] Fannie's portfolio did not accurately reflect the risk it had accumulated, and eventually Fannie began "internally develop[ing] its own unique methodology" for accounting and risk assessment, factors that led to its 2004 earnings restatement.[66] The restatement would distract Fannie's attention away from market changes and into meticulous accounting in the mid-2000s, yet another problematic outcome in the wake before the Great Recession.

4.2. Pathway to Politics

A Federal Reserve Bank of Boston study in 1992 entitled "Mortgage Lending in Boston: Interpreting HMDA Data"[67] revealed that mortgage lenders in Boston, and presumably the rest of the nation, were more inclined to deny mortgage loans to Hispanic and African American applicants than whites in comparable financial situations. Even with similar financials—FICO score, annual income—banks were 60% more likely to turn down minority mortgage applicants than whites.[68] The study reverberated through the entire mortgage industry as minority nonprofits groups like the NAACP, the Leadership Conference on Civil Rights, and the National Urban League began demanding change from Fannie and Freddie.

The study instigated a major public relations nightmare for Fannie, which began promising to promote equal access to minorities. Critics claimed Fannie gave lenders too much discretion in their lending practices and was not actively following through with lower-income purchases. When fulfilling HUD requirements, Fannie would buy whatever the mortgage originator classified as "lower-income purchases" without any verification of nondiscriminatory lending practices. Thus, through its inaction, Fannie indirectly supported prejudiced mortgage lending toward blacks, Hispanics, and other minority groups.

Soon Fannie announced measures to play an increasingly active role in lower-income mortgage purchases. In 1994, it would also declare a trillion-dollar initiative to finance housing for minorities and low- and moderate-income families. Pattye Green, a senior business manager at Fannie, commented on Fannie's vision to support minority housing by the decade's end through the Trillion Dollar Commitment: "In 1994, we made a commitment to provide $1 trillion in financing for 10 million, serve 10 million underserved families, low- and moderate-income families, minorities, and new Americans, as well as residents of central cities and urban areas."[69]

The same year Fannie promised a localized investment of over $750 million in Baltimore to support affordable housing.[70] Jim Johnson, Fannie's president, visited the city, touring neighborhoods and holding press conferences with local congressmen Paul Sarbanes and Kweisi Mfume. Similar promises of investment and urbanization followed in cities throughout the nation, including New Orleans, Columbus, and Chicago. Johnson eventually opened up "Partnership Offices" in nearly all 50 states: localized Fannie offices dedicated to improving affordable housing in metropolitan areas. Fannie spent millions on each office annually and began a national homeownership advertising campaign that would run well into the mid-2000s, averaging an additional $40 million in annual expenses.[71]

Initially, Fannie appeared to genuinely improve its tarnished reputation. Specifically, the homeownership advertising campaign was less "educational than an image-burnishing effort."[72] Another gimmick, to become a sponsor of the National Basketball Association, seemed exactly that—a quick public-relations play. Yet Fannie's investments in the Partnership Offices seemed unsubstantiated: the profitability associated with supporting lower-income housing did not match Fannie's volume of invested capital in its new projects. Fannie Mae's fallback reason in defending any homeownership measure, the HUD lower-income purchase requirements, did not seem to suffice.

The Partnership Offices, promoted as business arms to support homeownership, actually served as part-business, part-political operations. Fannie had strategically chosen office locations to match with influential Congress members' districts, essentially setting up a plethora of grassroots lobbying arms. Politicians contributed "laudable quotes" for Fannie's press releases and benefited from the economic impacts of Fannie's urban housing investments in their districts.[73] Meanwhile, if Fannie needed help to oppose or weaken legislation, like H.R. 5640: The American Homeownership and Economic Opportunity Act of 2000 or H.R. 1461: The Federal Housing Finance Reform Act of 2005, a few Congress members would be willing to help out. A decision to impose stricter capital requirements on Fannie and Freddie, for example, was rejected by a House subcommittee vote of 49:1. Representative Jim Leach of Iowa, the sole dissenter, commented on the increasingly difficult nature of opposing Fannie Mae, saying that although his Iowa constituents "paid no attention to debates about regulations, whenever he defied [Fannie], he heard from irate Realtors, home builders, and advocates for housing projects."[74] Attempting to restrict Fannie was a lost cause, and the few Congress members who were asking too many questions, such as Representative Richard Baker of Louisiana and Representative Mike Oxley of Ohio, faced fears of losing reelection.

Fannie Mae's Partnership Offices had set up a grassroots lobbying network that was "considered among the most sophisticated and extensive in America, exceeding even the storied programs of AT&T and a range of military contractors."[75] Ultimately, Fannie had utilized its efforts to support lower-income and minority housing as a facade to hide intentions of supporting American homeownership measures for the sake of shareholders, not for the benefit of lower-income families seeking to buy homes. Fannie had reshaped the intended purpose of the mandatory HUD requirements to justify its expanded measures and in doing so had set up a powerful lobbying network in Washington DC, ready to prevent any attempts at meaningful regulation. Fannie CEO Franklin D. Raines, coincidentally named after FNMA founder President Roosevelt, later testified in Congress about Fannie's minority pledge:

[In 2000], we launched a pledge to provide $2 trillion for 18 million underserved families...we are one of the best-capitalized financial institutions in the world.

—Franklin Raines, CEO of Fannie Mae, 1999–2004[76]

5. FALTERING BUSINESS MODEL

5.1. The New Guaranty Business

David O. Maxwell became the president of Fannie Mae just as Ronald Reagan was sworn in as president of the United States. In 1981 Fannie held about $64.8 billion in mortgages.[77] Its business model involved buying mortgages from originators (using borrowed money at extremely low interest rates) and receiving the homeowners' monthly mortgage payments. Fannie would profit from the difference between its low borrowing costs and the homeowners' higher mortgage rates. In late 1981, however, Fannie introduced another aspect to its business model: a guaranty arm. Similar to an insurance policy, Fannie would not purchase the mortgage outright from the originator but would guarantee the mortgage with its special government backing. If the homeowner defaulted, Fannie would step in and cover the losses for the investors.[78] Fannie charged its g-fee for its service.

The guaranty business caught on fast. Fannie guaranteed $20 billion worth of mortgages in its first year, about 25% of its total portfolio.[79] It enjoyed a period of uninterrupted growth from 1980 to 1986, with total portfolio growth from $56 billion to $94 billion.[80] Although the guaranty arm functioned profitably in good economic conditions, Fannie would have to be ready to bear the brunt of mass foreclosures. The Reagan Administration allowed the guaranty business to flourish. Although President Reagan funded 300-page reports on the state of the nation's housing, he largely ignored Fannie's new strategy: "the genius of the market economy, freed from housing regulation, can provide for housing better than federal programs."[81] If anything, Reagan reasoned, Fannie's implicit government guarantee would be able to resolve any complications of a free market vision.

5.2. Capital Requirements Popularize Securitization

In addition to the development of a guaranty arm, the other pivotal change in Fannie's business model was its introduction of mortgage-backed securities in 1981. The process of securitization (explored earlier in "The Secret Lives of Residential Mortgages") simply refers to the act of gathering guaranteed mortgages and organizing them into similar bundles, or pools, which can then be sold and traded among different financial institutions. Throughout the 1980s the securitization market remained largely dormant and experimental; it was only after President George H. W. Bush passed the aforementioned FHEFSSA in 1992 that the securitization market emerged into a scalable endeavor.

While FHEFSSA compounded the rivalry between Fannie Mae and the HUD, another aspect of Bush's legislation included a framework for implementing capital requirements for the GSEs (Fannie and Freddie)[82] and other related housing institutions as a safeguard for the new guaranty business. Fannie was required to hold a 0.45% capital buffer for securitized and guaranteed mortgages and a 2.5% buffer when investing in MBSs. Banks, on the other hand, received stronger capital requirements of 4%[83] for holding a portfolio of mortgages. Yet if banks held Fannie MBSs, that requirement was lowered to only 1.6%.[84] Thus, a shortcut was cleverly crafted. Mortgage originators could originate $100 of mortgages and then be required to have $4 in capital. But, if Fannie Mae bought these loans, guaranteed them, and securitized them into MBSs, the originator could sell them to investors at a slightly higher price, say $103 (depending, of course, on the market price). Then the investors needed to hold only $103 x 1.6% = $1.65 in capital—much less than the original $100 x 4% = $4. Meanwhile, the mortgage originator made its cut by selling the MBSs at slightly higher prices ($103 compared to $100), and Fannie profited from its guaranty fee. When dealing with only hundreds of dollars, the 4% vs. 1.6% requirement does not appear as a significant loophole, but with billions and even trillions of dollars, borrowing can easily get out of hand, and capital may not be readily available if enough investments sour. With the incentives to buy securitized mortgages for investors and the incentives to securitize for Fannie Mae, the secondary mortgage market was truly born. A system of buying and selling mortgage-backed securities and bonds would come to blossom among broker-dealers, hedge funds, banks, the Federal Reserve, and even the GSEs.

The securitization market radically changed the mortgage landscape. Mortgage lenders became less concerned with trading singular loans, as the mortgage business became less about personal relationships and more about "high-volume transactions."[85] Soon, annual MBS issuance grew from $250 billion in 1990 to $700 billion in 1998 and eventually to $2 trillion in 2005.[86] The securitization market, largely blamed for the mortgage crisis in 2008, had its roots in a loophole in the FHEFSSA over fifteen years prior. It was primarily securitization of private-label mortgages—not GSE mortgages—that led to the problems at Lehman Brothers and others.

5.3. The "Fannie-Mae Standard"

Since 1970 the GSEs had enjoyed a monopoly-like reputation in the mortgage sector. Fannie engaged in guaranteeing, purchasing, and securitizing mortgages. Together, Fannie's guarantee policy and implicit government backing created a low-risk endeavor for mortgage originators. Likewise, when MBS bonds were sold to investors, the risk of investors losing money due to mortgage default was also very low.[87] Reflecting the associated low risk, Fannie Mae MBS bonds had low yields: investors would not receive outstandingly high returns on Fannie's bonds. Thus, investors viewed its bonds not as risky play to generate a lot of money but as an alternative to depositing large sums of money in a savings bank. Low risk transformed Fannie Mae MBS bonds into an alternative that was almost as safe as benchmark US Treasury bonds. Some investors argue Fannie's bonds were better investments because they came with slightly higher yields and a similar government guarantee. For the majority of the 2000s, Fannie Mae MBS bonds were the second-most issued bonds in America, trailing only US Treasury bonds.[88] Reflecting their remarkable issuance, Fannie Mae MBS bonds became synonymous with safety and security, allowing Fannie to be ingrained as a trusted name in the minds of Americans.

I'm fairly confident we're not [being] stupid.

We have a history of not doing anything stupid.

—Angelo Mozilo, founder and former CEO of Countrywide Financial[89]

6. THE CRISIS

6.1. The Rise

The early 2000s gave rise to new competition for Fannie and Freddie: private-label securitization (PLS). In order to compete with the government-sponsored giants, new private institutions would need to (a) obtain mortgage loans and (b) securitize the loans in the secondary mortgage market. Soon private companies aimed at subprime loans—mortgage loans that, legally, Fannie could not pursue.[90] Fannie Mae could only guarantee loans up to the "conforming" level, but without any substantial government involvement, the new competition approached the mortgage spectrum immune to Fannie Mae.

Private-label corporations incentivized their services through "teaser rates"—rates that would begin unnaturally low for a few years and spike up dramatically later (from 2% to 5%, for example). Private companies also encouraged mortgage refinancing[91], lower down payments (loan to home value LTV), and higher loan values. In 2007, the average down payment was only 9% of the home value, down from 20% in 1989. Additionally, an average 30% of homebuyers paid no money down in the mid-2000s.[92] Through these incentives, private-label companies gained market share in the mortgage market. In 1996 private-label mortgage originations represented 13% of annual mortgage originations, growing slowly to 18% in 2003 and rising rapidly to almost 50% in 2006.[93] As private-label originations jumped to more than $1 trillion in 2006,[94] Americans learned about their teaser rates and lower down payments, and private companies began eating away at the bread-and-butter homeowners Fannie Mae depended upon.

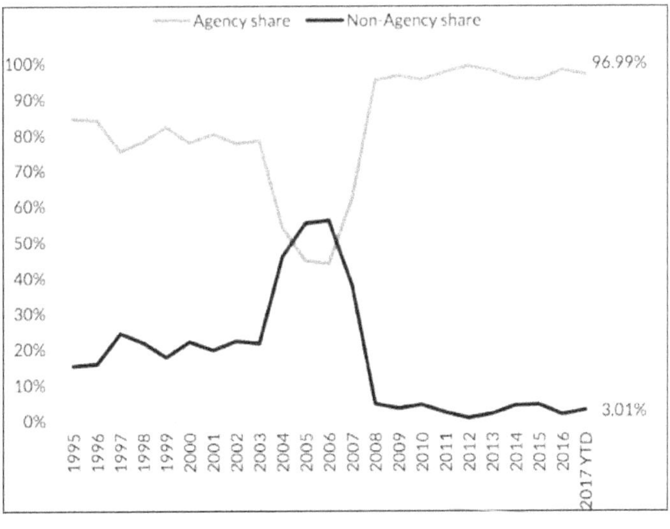

Figure 6.1: The Rise and Fall of PLS Securitization *(Source: Urban Institute)*

In the mid-2000s, as private-label originators secured their share of the market, they also began securitizing their mortgages by offering PLS bonds to investors. Unlike Fannie Mae MBS bonds, PLS mortgage bonds were *not* guaranteed: PLS bondholders could lose all of their money if the homebuyers they were dependent on defaulted. To make the risk more appealing, PLS created "tranching"[95] financial structure and advertised higher, more rewarding yields on their bonds, making it more profitable for investors to invest in PLS instead of Fannie Mae bonds. Investors looking for greater risk/reward dived into PLS mortgage bonds, attracted by higher rates of return. In 2006, almost 80% of private-label mortgage originations were securitized, up from 50% in 2001, reflecting investors' growing appetite for higher risk/reward.[96] Even Fannie and Freddie joined the PLS bandwagon, acquiring almost 40% of PLS purchases in 2004.[97]

Still, most investors required risk assessments on PLS bonds to receive a third-party verification on the chances of bond failure. Risk-rating agencies (companies like S&P, Fitch, and Moody's) assessed risk on PLS bonds following issuance.[98] As the private companies targeted subprime borrowers, the set of homebuyers outside Fannie Mae's reach, rating agencies would be expected to consider the low FICO scores, higher LTVs, and weaker incomes when determining PLS bond ratings. Notwithstanding subprime characteristics, ratings on many PLS bonds were near the perfect "AAA" status, indicating that perhaps ratings were inflated. For their work, rating agencies received generous consulting fees from the institutions.[99] Clearly, moral hazard was at play.

As analyzed in "The Secret Lives of Residential Mortgages" section, MBSs are traded among a plethora of financial institutions. In the early 2000s, PLS securities were an addition into this market, which eventually, with the inflated ratings and increased investor confidence, became an integral component. By 2007, investment banks, insurance firms, private originators, and even the GSEs developed a simple methodology to trade PLS and MBSs: rolling loans. Institutions took out new bonds to pay for existing bonds, with the short-term money financing a pipeline of capital to purchase, securitize, and trade any PLS and MBS available. With investor interest and excitement, this system of mortgage trading thrived. Nevertheless, the secondary mortgage market was only as healthy as the institutions comprising it, and the PLS companies, for which the foundation was primarily subprime homeowners, were becoming increasingly large players.

6.2. Homeowners

While private companies and MBS investors enjoyed large returns, homeowners, too, benefited from a de-monopolizing of the mortgage market. PLS institutions began further lowering standards and offering more teaser rates, allowing more Americans to buy homes. Homeownership rates rose from 64.7% in 1995 to 69% in 2005,[100] a remarkable increase considering that during the previous ten years, from 1984 to 1994, the rate fluctuated between only 63.5–64.5%.[101] The homeownership increase caused a prolonged rise in home prices, which rose for an "unprecedented" 135 months in a row between 1995 and 2006.[102]

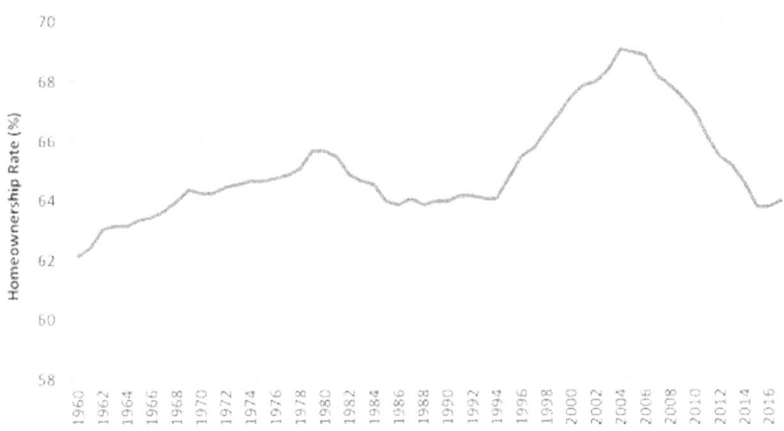

Figure 6.2: Historic Homeownership Rates *(Source: US Census)*

At first increased home prices only helped American homeowners: their LTV reduced dramatically. If a home was bought at $100,000 with a $10,000 down payment, the LTV was originally 90%. A few years later, if the home price rose to $120,000, the LTV improved to 75%. Homebuyers used this opportunity to extract money from their houses in the form of home equity lines of credit (HELOC). Homeowners used HELOC for home improvement projects, among other expenditures. These construction projects helped fuel the economic expansion in the mid-2000s; the additional money spent on homes stimulated the housing industry and in turn the economy.

Eventually, however, many homeowners were hurt by predatory lending practices. Existing homeowners enjoyed a false sense of financial stability. While their home prices rose, their incomes did not, creating an unsustainable situation for the economy. When the unrealistically low teaser rates reset into higher ones (the typical rate readjustment could double or triple monthly mortgages), homeowners struggled to keep up with rising mortgage payments. Worse, a highly disproportionate number of teaser rates were set to adjust in the span of 2007–2009.[103] The rate readjustment without the corresponding income growth triggered a wave of foreclosures that had rippling effects across the housing industry. Investors quickly realized the real risk of PLS and pulled out from PLS bonds.

6.3. Fannie Falls (Part One)

Initially for Fannie Mae, the private-label competition negatively impacted progress toward HUD mission goals. Fannie struggled to appeal to lower-income homeowners with the growth of private-label incentives and consequently delved into riskier mortgage loans. The impetus of the HUD's regulations would translate into reduced criteria for homebuyers and stretched conforming loan limits, revealing that HUD regulators had become blinded by the singularity of their mission to consider the larger context for Fannie's financial health. From 2001 to 2005, Fannie still failed to attract subprime borrowers, falling far short of the 30% HUD mandate to support urban housing, and fears grew until the HUD let Fannie to purchase large quantities of rival PLS securities, mainly ones given "AAA" ratings. In 2001 Fannie and Freddie purchased 4% of subprime issuance, peaking to 39% in 2004 and tapering to 25% in 2007.[104] Fannie's president at the time, Daniel Mudd, had convinced HUD regulators that PLS bond purchases supported Fannie's overarching mission of supporting lower-income housing.[105] Mudd argued that not only were PLS securities an alternative to direct purchases, but they were also much safer and had less risk and chance of loss. Convinced by and satisfied with Mudd's pitch, the HUD readily agreed.

However, another underlying factor hid behind Fannie's decision to purchase PLS bonds: profitability. Major portions of Fannie's revenue growth in the mid-2000s can be traced directly to private-label mortgage purchases. Mudd had taken advantage of the HUD's desire to support homeownership by opening new avenues of profit for Fannie's bottom line. Simply put, Mudd had aimed for stronger revenue streams, and ultimately fatter bonus checks, in the name of the HUD's housing sustainability motto. Mudd's negotiations demonstrate that despite its supposed public nature, Fannie was truly a money-oriented mortgage giant.

Fannie wound up losing billions when PLS bonds began failing but was able to deflect blame towards the HUD's supposed authorization of PLS purchases. The unresolved nature of the conflict between the HUD and Fannie, propagated for decades through forced mandates and unchecked lobbying, culminated in widespread losses. Had the HUD been given a defined role and proper regulatory power in Johnson's 1968 plan, a significant portion of Fannie's $46 billion PLS-related loss could have been saved in 2008.[106]

6.4. The Fall

The interconnectedness of the financial institutions led to their fast, destructive demise. As banks pulled out of PLS bonds, other institutions lost faith in the secondary mortgage market. These institutions, dependent on rolling loans and a steady pipeline of money, began defaulting on their loans due to investors' loss of confidence. Bear Stearns's disclosure of failed subprime hedge funds in July 2007 acted as the harbinger of the looming crisis. Furthermore, without investor interest in the market, PLS origination, securitization, and bond issuance completely collapsed!

Fannie Mae and Freddie Mac remained as the only options left to stimulate the housing sector. The seemingly endless supply of private-label cash driving securitization just months earlier had simply vanished. OFHEO, Fannie's regulator, let Fannie reposition itself as top player to save the entire mortgage market: the effects of a complete mortgage lending shutdown would be devastating to the economy. Consequently, Fannie and Freddie exploded; their total debt and MBSs outstanding were valued at $3.6 trillion in 2006 but had risen to $5.2 trillion in 2008.[107] Fannie Mae and Freddie regained control of the market they had developed. By the first quarter of 2008, Fannie and Freddie were guaranteeing 80% of mortgages, double their market share only two years prior.[108]

The Great Recession, the worst financial crisis to hit the world since the Great Depression, officially struck in early 2008. Fingers of blame pointed at the subprime market crisis and dumb regulation. For the next nineteen months, global markets would struggle, shedding between half and two-thirds of their value.

Although all Americans lost household equity and felt the pressures of the credit crunch,[109] minority borrowers felt it the most. Private-label corporations that had employed predatory lending practices disproportionately devastated black and Hispanic communities, often leading to increased health problems and suicide rates. A California survey found that Americans going through foreclosure were more than twice as likely to have mental and physical health deterioration (including increases in stress, depression, and anxiety) compared with those not going through foreclosure. Moreover, a 5% increase in real-estate foreclosures between 2005 and 2010 was associated with a 25% increase in the suicide rate for adults between the ages of 46 and 64.[110]

As home prices peaked in 2005 and 2006, increasingly skewed numbers of minorities entered the housing market. From 2001 to 2005, mortgage originations increased 102% for black homebuyers and 129% for Hispanics vs. a relatively modest 41% increase for whites. Following 2005, black and Hispanic mortgage purchases fell by 76% and 78%, respectively, compared with only 56% for whites.[111] The increasing minority foreclosure rates compounded the downturn in home prices. When private-label corporations debuted stricter credit standards and higher FICO score requirements in 2006 and 2007, the minority homeowners who had missed payments or foreclosed were effectively shut out of the market with weaker FICO scores. The correction in credit ratings had severely worsened mortgage accessibility for minorities.

6.5. Fannie Falls (Part Two)

With rampant foreclosures in 2007 and 2008, Fannie's guaranteed mortgages began failing in alarming numbers, and prospective default fears remained strong for the coming years. The weakly regulated and highly profitable guaranty arm would betray Fannie during this time of rising unemployment, plummeting home prices, and slowing economic activity. As millions of homeowners defaulted, banks came rushing to Fannie for their insurance payments. But Fannie had already spent the g-fee money on doomed PLS bonds and needed tremendous injections of capital to absorb its losses. It needed liquidity to deal with its maturing debt or it needed government backing to be able to refinance the debt: $250 billion in debt was scheduled to mature in less than a year, and against that Fannie held only $84 billion in capital.[112]

The fatally flawed "implicit" government backing had led to the Reagan Administration's acceptance of Fannie's guaranty arm, a business that had transformed from an additional revenue source into a cornerstone of Fannie's business model, accounting for nearly 53% of Fannie's income in 2007.[113] Fannie could no longer depend on its guaranty arm to provide profits, as the rising foreclosure rates foretold Fannie's obligation to cover losses for future mortgage defaults, essentially turning its profitable business into another source of loss. Although the guaranty business had successfully weathered two decades of relative housing stability, the Great Recession revealed its true nature: an unsustainable and unregulated burden. The "implicit" government backing had also led to a psychological impact in Fannie's offices.[114] Company memos and notices demonstrated a lack of urgency in the tones of executives, implying that Fannie's sponsorship had led to a corrosion of both moral principles and monetary decision-making standards.

6.6. Still in Conservatorship

Fannie and Freddie failing would be another catastrophic blow to not only American financial markets but also the global market.[115] In 2008, foreign nations, namely China, Japan, and Germany, owned $1.46 trillion of combined Fannie and Freddie debt, mainly because they believed the GSEs held a government guarantee.[116] Henry Paulson, Secretary of Treasury from 2006–2009, indicated his frustration at foreign investment in Fannie Mae: "Try to go around to one world leader after another and explain what this implicit-not-explicit government guarantee was about."[117] In addition to Fannie and Freddie debt, China and Japan also held $3.3 trillion (two-thirds) of US Treasury debt. With the reputation of the world's most powerful treasury at stake, Fannie Mae and Freddie Mac truly had become "too big to fail."[118] The government moved fast, enabling a 79.9% takeover of Fannie and Freddie in a multibillion-dollar bailout.[119] Fannie's executives were fired, and its stock was pulled from the NYSE, allowing a new regulator, the Federal Housing Finance Agency (FHFA), to begin life-support examination under a "conservatorship"—a period focused solely on repair and restructuring.[120]

The government clearly stated that during conservatorship, the GSEs were to be focused solely on repair—not on shareholder interests. The Treasury provided $187.5 billion in the form of a taxpayer-funded line of credit over the next four years with staggering 10% interest rates.[121] In addition, the government received preferred stock for its investments, meaning it would be paid back before any other investors received dividends. Ultimately, dividends were suspended altogether. By wiping out the voices of investors, the FHFA and the Treasury could focus on repairing the broken system. Reflecting on the decision to put Fannie and Freddie under government conservatorship, Paulson said it was the "most impactful, and gutsiest, thing we ever did."[122] Meanwhile, Fannie executives complained about the government's decision, claiming the government did not foresee, nor specify, a clear plan for the days ahead. Fannie's and Freddie's financial situations certainly did not make them popular; their crumbling positions provoked two responses: while the FHFA and Treasury tried reviving the GSEs, congressional bills outlined their end.

The original form of the bailout was senior preferred stock with a 10% dividend. But in 2013, by an agreement between the FHFA and the Treasury, the dividend was changed from the original 10% to essentially 100% of the net profit in a notorious "profit sweep." Fannie and Freddie have cumulatively paid $280 billion in total dividends to the Treasury, about 47% more than the original bailout package.[123] Even today, ten years post-2008, Fannie and Freddie still remain under government conservatorship.

Letting [the GSEs] fail would have been catastrophic.

It would have been worse than [another] Great Depression.

—Henry Paulson, Secretary of Treasury, 2006–2009[124]

Too big to fail…

—Andrew Sorkin, author of *Too Big to Fail*[125]

7. PROPOSAL REVIEW

While in conservatorship, the fates of Fannie and Freddie have been the source of much speculation among economists, investors, and politicians. In the early years after the Great Recession, Congress attempted to both revive the slumped housing sector and extend support to the GSEs through the Home Affordable Refinance Program (HARP). Enacted in 2009 and reintroduced in 2012, the HARP helped struggling homeowners to refinance[126] mortgages. To qualify, the homeowner must have had a mortgage guaranteed by Fannie Mae or Freddie Mac. Ultimately, the HARP not only helped the GSEs recover money (Fannie Mae posted a profit in the fourth quarter of 2011) but also aided nearly 2 million Americans in refinancing their mortgages.[127] Meanwhile, FHFA director Edward DeMarco was keen to raise the GSEs' guaranty fee not only to help in Fannie's and Freddie's recovery but also to help taxpayers. In December 2011, President Obama signed into law H.R. 3630, a measure that sought to increase the guaranty fee for the next ten years. Indeed, guaranty fees tripled between 2009 and 2013.[128] Most of the additional revenue generated from the fee increase went straight to the Treasury, funding corporate tax cuts![129] The 2010 Dodd-Frank law also increased the federal government's regulatory oversight on financial markets. Tighter regulations, which ex-Fannie executives particularly loathed, were safeguards against another financial crisis by allowing for better transparency and risk assessment.

7.1. Attempted Reforms

7.1.1. The Corker-Warner and Johnson-Crapo Bills

While the Treasury and the FHFA sought Fannie and Freddie revival, Congress made several attempts to shut down the costly GSEs, effectively removing any government involvement from the mortgage market. Introduced to Congress in 2013, the Corker-Warner bill became a landmark proposition concerning the fate of the GSEs. Unlike previous attempts to completely eliminate the government from the mortgage market, the Corker-Warner bill laid guidelines to an alternative institution. Two senators, Democrat David Warner of Virginia and Republican Bob Corker of Tennessee, wanted to abolish the GSEs within a five-year period and replace them with two private insurers. The new system of insurers would be required to readily have capital to cover 10% of losses as well as pay a fee to the government for explicitly backing them during times of crisis. The bill, which had several bipartisan cosponsors, died in the Senate.[130] Conveniently, Fannie Mae began paying back the Treasury, starting with a $59 billion dividend in May 2013. By December 2014, Fannie Mae had cumulatively paid back the Treasury $134.5 billion in dividends—approximately $18 billion more than it had received in support.[131] Nonetheless, GSE reform bills persisted.

The 2014 Johnson-Crapo bill heavily reiterated the Corker-Warner bill but contained several distinct features. The GSEs themselves would not receive any government guarantee, but the government would instead guarantee MBSs for a fee. Moreover, the Johnson-Crapo bill suggested much stronger capital requirements of 10% for trading MBSs. While the Corker-Warner and Johnson-Crapo bills formed a strong foundation for future proposals, both contained unfortunate similarities with the existing mortgage system, most notably an explicit federal guarantee on MBSs.

7.1.2. The New York Federal Reserve and Milken Institute Plans

A plan proposed by economists at the New York Federal Reserve in 2010 called for Fannie Mae and Freddie Mac to be replaced by a financial market utility that would be mutually owned by institutions involved in mortgage lending. This utility would securitize mortgages into MBSs and guarantee their default risk but set prices on MBSs independently (although still subject to government regulation). The government would have no involvement in this utility, but the lack of specificity toward the extent of regulations churned concern for another lobbying nightmare. The proposal also included measures for an explicit, government reinsurance guarantee against catastrophic loss.

In 2016 former FHFA director Edward DeMarco led a similar initiative from the Milken Institute. His proposal amends GSEs charters to organize Fannie and Freddie into lender-owned mutual funds. The GSEs would have no government support other than the delegation of a credit enhancer. However, the concept of mutual ownership, although essential in providing credit support for MBSs, remains untested in a severe economic downturn, causing speculation about survival and proper functioning during recessions.

7.2. Risk Sharing

The most significant change impacting post-bailout Fannie Mae has been risk sharing. In order to adequately protect against credit risk, or the risk of a homeowner defaulting, Fannie Mae was pushed to develop several avenues that would lower taxpayer liability. Beginning in 2013, Fannie ramped up sales of a new type of MBS, which it calls "Connecticut Avenue Securities" (CASs),[132] with higher yields that reflect potential losses to investors. The FHFA, led by Mel Watt, ultimately aimed to transfer most of the risk on Fannie Mae's future guarantees to investors instead of taxpayers. Fannie serves as an intermediary between lenders and investors by "setting standards, providing credit risk management oversight, and maintaining stability through business cycles."[133] Fannie's risk-sharing initiatives offer increased transparency to investors, marked by easily accessible data, resources, and tools. The FHFA mandated that Fannie securitize a considerable amount of newly acquired mortgages as CASs. Since 2013 Fannie has brought 24 CAS deals to market, issued $30 billion in notes, and transferred a portion of credit risk to private investors on about $1 trillion worth of residential mortgage loans through the CAS program. Most recently, Fannie announced a $1.148 billion CAS deal in early February 2017, the eighth such deal that year.[134] CAS transactions currently comprise nearly 35% of Fannie's overall book of business.[135]

Fixing Fannie in isolation, without looking at the big picture, would be short sighted.

—Bethany McLean, Shaky Ground: The Strange Saga of the U.S. Mortgage Giants[136]

8. RECOMMENDATIONS

Fannie Mae's past details the perpetual creeping of homeownership policies into shareholders' wishes. Decades of lobbying and manipulating HUD goals ensured weak business model regulation, allowing uninhibited and unchecked expansion. Yet even with a tremendous fall in the Great Recession in 2008, Fannie remains a keystone of the mortgage market, housing sector, and entire American economy. In 2016 Fannie and Freddie issued a combined $992 billion in MBSs, signaling their enduring relevance.[137] Although the secondary market between the GSEs and private institutions operates smoothly under stable economic conditions, it can be put under great stress in an economic downturn, creating a massive liability for the GSEs and the government and eventually burdening taxpayers.

Fortunately, Fannie's history offers insights for policy recommendations. The "Privatization" and "Politics and Profits" sections detailed conflicting housing ideologies. Although the HUD guidelines aimed to benefit the population, Fannie misused mandates to justify faulty actions, such as endeavoring into risky profitability and launching grassroots lobbying networks. The "Faltering Business Model" and "The Crisis" sections demonstrated how "dumb regulation" allowed Fannie to transform into a mortgage behemoth, playing a role in bringing about the Great Recession. Ultimately, reforms need to reduce Fannie's outstanding liability on taxpayers while continuing to support American homeownership measures.

8.1. Mitigating Taxpayer Liability

The ultimate goal relating to the GSEs should be winding down the government's involvement in mortgages through the use of completely private yet thoughtfully regulated enterprises. This outcome necessitates a twofold agenda to reduce Fannie's liability: (a) reducing Fannie's role in the mortgage market and (b) introducing self-sustaining private enterprises.

8.1.1. Reducing Fannie's Role

In order to lessen Fannie's outstanding liability, its role in the marketplace should be gradually reduced. Specific avenues to reduce its size (and therefore its liability) are summarized in Table 8.1.

Reform	Mechanism
Shrink Fannie Mae's mortgage portfolio.	Adjust Fannie's annual asset limit of $288 billion to a lower value.
Reduce Fannie Mae's reliance on GSE status.	Increase federal taxes on profits from Fannie's guaranty arm.
Strengthen Fannie Mae's regulator.	Augment the budgetary funds and congressional mandate of the FHFA.

Table 8.1: Reducing Fannie's Footprint in Mortgages

The most effective method to limit Fannie's growth would be to shrink its mortgage portfolio. Currently, Fannie has regulatory requirements of an annual asset accumulation cap of $288 billion.[138] Fannie continues to not only meet but also pursue an average of 5% decrease in annual investments.[139] Its sustained cooperation suggests that the accumulation cap can be further reduced to, say, $250 billion. Imposing a stricter asset limit would reduce Fannie Mae's debt obligations and allow it to liquidate holdings, slowly dissolving its footprint in the mortgage market.

Additionally, Fannie's problematic reliance on its government-sponsorship status should be gradually reduced. The guaranty business can shift from a profitable moneymaker to an overwhelming money-drainer extremely quickly. A sharp increase in government taxes on the g-fee can facilitate and encourage Fannie to shift away from its guaranty book of business.

Last, strengthening Fannie Mae's regulator would allow for greater transparency. Increasing both the budget and the congressional mandate of the FHFA would result in a better-managed Fannie, lessening the likelihood of corporate misgovernance, manipulation of HUD intentions, and potential earnings restatements. Fannie would be pushed toward greater accountability, preventing excessive lobbying and compensation procedures. Ultimately, a stronger regulator would not alleviate Fannie's monetary burden but would result in a more efficient and "ready-for-reform" organization. It is important to note, however, that additional channels of dialogue between the HUD and the FHFA should be created in order to prevent conflicts of interest within the government itself.

8.1.2. Creating Private Enterprises

While Fannie and Freddie are being wound down, new private enterprises can fill the void in the mortgage markets and lessen the GSEs' liability.[140] The root source of risk in the mortgage market is one clear factor: home foreclosure. Therefore, any measure to address the financial health of Fannie and Freddie should mitigate the risks of foreclosure on the mortgage system. On that premise, this proposal would facilitate the creation of one or more "Private Servicer Enterprises" (PSEs) in the secondary mortgage market. Before understanding the functions of the PSE, it is necessary to revisit the process associated with mortgage default from "The Secret Lives of Residential Mortgages" section:

1. The parameter to determine foreclosure likelihood in the secondary mortgage market is the 120-day delinquency point, which indicates the homeowner has fallen behind on four monthly mortgage payments.
2. At this stage, delinquent loans are removed from the MBS bond into the GSE's balance sheet. The GSE, according to its guaranty

business, compensates the MBS investors with an up-front payment of the remaining mortgage loan value.

3. The MBS bond investors are financially unaffected by the homeowner delinquency.

8.1.3. PSE Function

1. The introduction of the PSEs would considerably reduce the risk on this system. PSEs would have the sole purpose of servicing the 120-day delinquent mortgages from the GSE. Moreover, PSEs would have no government backing, operating independently but with prudent regulation.
2. At the 120-day delinquent status, the mortgage's servicer would introduce the PSE.
3. The PSE would coordinate a restructured mortgage contract between the homeowner and GSE. The terms of the modified contract would be facilitated by the PSE such that the homeowner would be able keep his or her home:
    a. The loan modification for the homeowner would involve monthly payments being reduced by a "y" % during an "x" year time frame to mitigate the homeowner's financial hardships.
    b. The contract length would receive an extension of those "x" number of years to compensate the GSE's contribution to monthly payments.
    c. Example: The PSE modifies the loan such that the homeowner's monthly payments are reduced 50% for the next five years, meaning the GSE will cover the remaining 50% for those five years. If the homeowner has already paid seven years of the original 30-year contract and has 23 years of payments left, then the newly modified contract would become a 35-year contract with 28 years left.
4. The PSE would collect the joint payment from the homeowner and GSE, sending the payment to the original servicer.
5. The original servicer would process the payment and forward the money to the investors in the specific MBS bond. The loan would not be transferred to the GSE portfolio but would remain with the MBS bond.
6. The MBS investors would remain financially unaffected by the delinquency, receiving monthly staggered payments *instead* of a single, upfront payment for the delinquent loan.

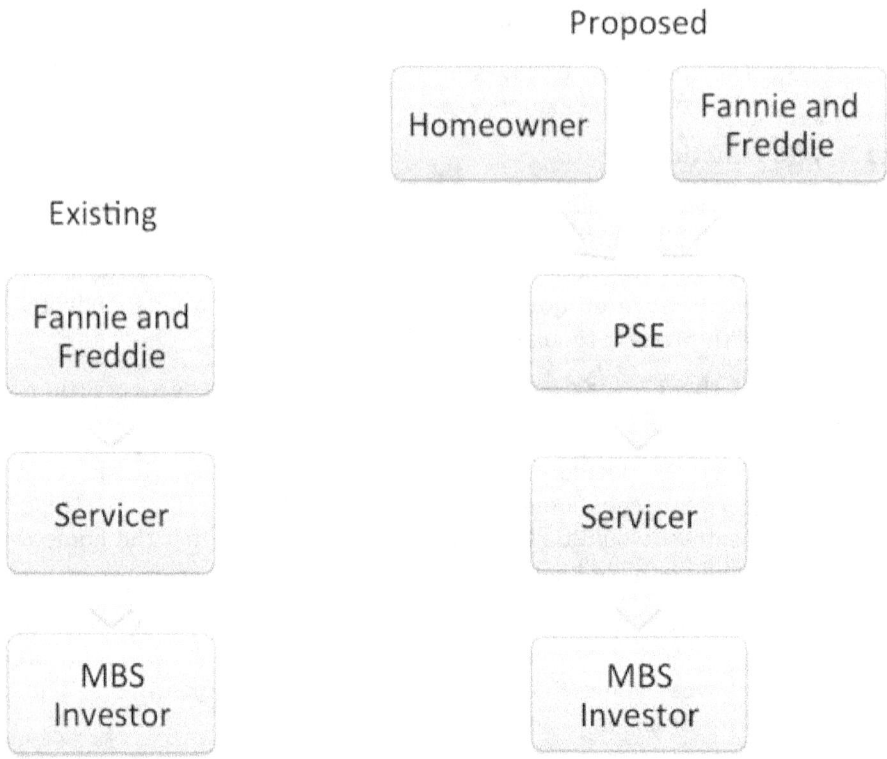

Figure 8.1: Transaction Flowchart of the Existing and Proposed Systems of Handling 120-Day Mortgage Delinquent Loans in MBS Bonds

8.1.4. PSE Operation

Procedure

Upon notification from the original servicer on 120-day delinquent loans, the PSE would now begin contact with the homeowner and the GSE. Primarily, the PSE would be responsible for forming an agreement between the GSE and homeowner on the mortgage modification. This would entail numerous correspondences between the two parties through email, phone, video, and in-person conversations. Additionally, the PSE would process and forward the joint payment back to the original servicer. Costs associated with PSE operation would be relatively low.

Incentive

The PSE would be incentivized from two potential revenue streams: charging (a) service fees and (b) marginal fees from the GSE. The PSE servicing fees would be comparable to the average servicing fee (which range from 0.25% for fixed-rate mortgages and 0.5% for adjustable-rate mortgages[141]) but sufficient to compensate PSE endeavors. The GSE would also pay the PSE a fee (similar to the average GSE guaranty fee of 0.57%) for reducing its potential loss on delinquent loans.

Regulation

The PSE would need to have sufficient regulatory oversight from both the consumer and government perspectives. The Consumer Financial Protection Bureau, a government agency responsible for consumer protection in the financial realm, would develop guidelines and procedures to (a) ensure homeowners were not mistreated or coerced into unjust modified contracts and (b) maintain that GSEs and PSE acted honorably during consumer interactions. Meanwhile, in order to avoid a conflict of preexisting interests under an existing government agency such as the HUD or the FHFA, a new government regulator would be created to oversee the PSE. The new regulator would act to (a) ensure homeowners did not abuse the mortgage modification system and misrepresent financial information for the purposes of receiving "free" subsidies and (b) investigate the PSEs' financials and accounting methods.

Creation

An existing financial institution, such as a commercial bank, private equity firm, or hedge fund, would create a PSE book of business to house PSE operations. Multiple PSEs could eventually exist, enhancing free market principles and competition.

8.1.5. PSE Benefits and Drawbacks

GSE Liability

This proposal would significantly reduce GSE liability by limiting the capital drain caused by homeowner default. Fannie's guaranty arm failed when, swamped with rampant foreclosures, Fannie had no available capital to make large, immediate payments to the mortgage investors. This proposal alters the nature of the loss coverage: instead of a single lump sum, Fannie's payments would be staggered monthly. In 2010, when Fannie experienced a serious delinquency rate of almost 14% and Freddie experienced one of over 9%,[142] Fannie's payout policy severely impacted its bottom line. Its guarantee and government sponsorship become problematic only when the housing market turns and necessitates such capital drain.

Moreover, with the speculation concerning the economy and the government's housing policies, a mechanism must protect the government, and ultimately taxpayers, from the burden of economic downturn. Serious delinquency rates currently hover around 1.5%,[143] but a quick escalation in delinquency rates translates into a dramatic monetary drain. Without modified policy, Fannie and Freddie would have to otherwise inject tremendous capital to protect investors in times of frequent foreclosures and recession (as they had to in 2008, thus forcing a $187.5 billion bailout). To further quantify the GSEs' current liability, the FHFA continues to perform legally required stress tests on Fannie and Freddie. Recent reports indicate that under a "severely adverse" economic scenario,[144] Fannie and Freddie would need as much as $100 billion in bailout money.[145] Clearly, the risks associated with GSE liability continue to threaten taxpayers.

Capital Requirements

The restructured payment (part homeowner, part Fannie) would also significantly improve the GSEs' future loss estimation capital requirement. Modified loans would have a lower chance of default compared to delinquent non-modified loans, and because the loans would not enter Fannie's portfolio, Fannie would not be required to hold as much capital in safeguard. For example, while Fannie's 0.45% capital requirements are applied to a mortgage expected to lose $100 (meaning that Fannie is required to hold $100 x .45% = $0.45 in capital), the modified payment structure would reduce the loss estimation to $0 because the troubled loans would not be held in Fannie's accounts. Yet some capital requirement should still remain, such as a 0.25% guideline that would require Fannie to hold $50 x .25% = $0.125.

Supporting Homeownership

This proposal would maintain socioeconomic stability by supporting homeownership measures. The modified payment structure would offer homeowners a new pathway to keep their homes. Additionally, formal foreclosures would be avoided, leading to less home price fluctuations in neighborhoods.

Reducing Systemic Risk

This proposal would greatly reduce the systemic risk of the mortgage market. Considering the interconnectedness of the secondary mortgage market, further stability among the various other financial institutions—including banks, funds, trusts, and all major holders of MBSs—would be cultivated. Additionally, by deferring the immediate impact of delinquent homeowners on the activities of MBS trading and the secondary mortgage market, a slight disconnect between the occurrences of the primary and secondary mortgages would be established.

In times of a potential crisis, this disconnect would allow think tanks, Congress, and government officials much-needed time to draft and revise a thoughtful but implantable government policy. A potential housing crisis would be much more easily traced, as the impacts of delinquencies would foreshadow potential difficulties in MBS trading.

Drawbacks

Although this proposal tackles the problematic nature of the implicit guarantee through an adjusted loan destination and modified payment method, and reduces the GSEs' outstanding liability on taxpayers, a few drawbacks certainly exist. First, the collective execution of the various facets—the PSE, the homeowner, Fannie and Freddie, the original servicer, and the investors—would be a strenuous endeavor. Strict legal and financial accounting would be required, but a smooth and speedy flow of communication and interactions between the involved parties would present a challenge. Second, chances of implementation would be difficult under the current political climate and congressional situation. With a divide on every major issue from immigration to tax reform, an attempt to reform housing would certainly be no different. The glut of attempted reform, from the Corker-Warner bill in 2013 to various think-tank proposals, also suggests reform passage would be difficult. Last, although this proposal shrinks Fannie's role in the mortgage and housing sector, the proposal does not fully privatize Fannie Mae into a shareholder company. Considering that Fannie's most recent quarterly report indicated a net income of $3.2 billion and a payment of $2.8 billion in dividends to the US Treasury in June 2017,[146] Fannie appears to be a financially healthy corporation ready to issue shareholder dividends.

8.2. Alternative Pathways of Supporting Homeownership

While a benefit of the PSE would be giving homeowners a pathway to keep their homes, alternative actions can also support homeownership. Since American homeownership's economic benefits and societal purpose remain a contentious topic in the present day, the concept of homeownership should be further evaluated. Homeownership rates have consistently fallen from a peak of 69% in the mid-2000s to below 64% in 2017, levels comparable to the 1960s.

With a total of 117 million owner and renter households and an estimated 10.6 million additional new households by 2020, the housing system is insufficient for the needs of the growing population.[147] Fannie's history suggests that the conflict between public and private interests when supporting homeownership is both inevitable and problematic.

Lobbying can render unsound regulations useless, and congressional mandates can be misconstrued to justify negligent action. Specifically, direct reforms can have a stronger impact in growing mortgage access and reducing discrimination in the housing market. American homeownership can be better supported by (a) restricting discriminatory lending practices and (b) increasing overall housing and mortgage availability. Proposed measures are summarized in Table 8.2.

Reform	**Mechanism**
Improve access to housing programs for all racial and ethnic groups.	Penalize wrongdoing with stricter measures, fund third-party studies to detect discrimination, and expand the HUD's budget.
Expand avenues in increasing mortgage and housing availability.	Expand the Community Reinvestment Act and update neighborhood codes.

Table 8.2: Reform Proposals to Support American Homeownership

8.2.1. Restricting Discriminatory Lending Practices

Although significant progress has been made for minority households, lending discrimination remains a prevalent crisis. The 1992 Federal Reserve of Boston report on mortgage lending was the first to formally cite the housing sector's discrimination of minorities. Government officials were shocked to learn that banks were 60% more likely to turn down minority mortgage applicants than white ones.

Although Fannie was eventually confronted for supporting similar measures, its response was lackluster: promises of trillion-dollar investment for a good PR campaign and the establishment of a grassroots lobbying network. Moreover, minority homebuyers were disproportionately disadvantaged during the 2008 housing bubble and credit crunch.

The mortgage system has played an undeniable role in America's racial wealth gap. Property ownership translates into better public schools and better chances of a college education. Properties serve as a hedge against rent increases and as collateral for financial investments. Yet racially restrictive lending and real estate practices systematically reduce access to homeownership (and neighborhood choice) for African American, Hispanic, Jewish, and Asian households. The effects of housing discrimination are passed down generationally, as previous generations' limited access and exclusion reduces opportunities for intergenerational wealth transfer and result in long-term disadvantage. Fannie Mae's central role in housing finance creates a conduit that, coupled with meaningful cooperation from the HUD, can rectify mortgage malpractice against minorities.

Imposing stricter penalties on wrongdoing would dramatically incentivize mortgage lenders to ensure nondiscriminatory lending procedures. On average, black borrowers continue to pay mortgage rates more than a quarter-point higher than comparable white borrowers. Regional banks, like Hudson City Bancorp in New Jersey and Bancorp South in Mississippi, were recently given $30 million[148] and $10 million[149] fines for discrimination, respectively. A similar but uniform national structure should be pursued. In addition, third-party studies can be funded to determine and detect instances of wrongdoing.

Additionally, an enlargement of the HUD's budget would allow for an expansion of already successful measures and the introduction of new policy. The HUD can fund improved housing finance literacy programs through both online initiatives and programs at regional offices, ensuring that first-time homebuyers make educated and informed decisions. An Urban Institute survey showed that 80% of consumers are either unaware of lenders' requirements for a down payment or believe that all lenders require a down payment above 5%.[150] The HUD prevails as the best resource to educate homebuyers and prevent predatory lending practices. In addition to educational outreach, the HUD should continue to pursue affordable housing programs. Historically, the Low-Income Housing Tax Credit has incentivized the creation of affordable housing in urban communities. Considering that housing cost burden is experienced more rampantly by minorities than whites—25% of black households, 22% of Hispanic households, and 19% of Asian households were severely cost burdened[151] compared with just 13% of white households in 2015[152]—HUD investments in affordable housing measures would have an increased impact on minority housing. Growth in the number of US households is now projected to reach 13.6 million in 2015–2025, roughly in line with the increase in the 1990s. Minority home purchases have the potential to contribute almost 75% of these gains, and thus avenues of increasing mortgage access to minorities are essential.[153]

8.2.2. Increasing Mortgage and Housing Availability

Fannie Mae's passive attempts to support lower-income housing, such as PLS bond purchases, serve as a reminder to demonstrate how easily policy intentions can be misconstrued. It is imperative for American housing policy to strive toward greater mortgage and housing availability. The majority of prospective homebuyers remain concerned with draining down payments, tightening credit standards, and waning affordability. Although there are more than 2,100 mortgage-assistance programs offered by more than 1,200 mortgage agencies throughout the nation,[154] additional supply-and-demand side measures need to support increased mortgage flow to Americans.

On the demand side, the Community Reinvestment Act (CRA) can be reformed and expanded to meet the housing need. The CRA essentially requires mortgage lenders to lend at an extent that would meet the needs of their surrounding communities, serving as a crucial motivator for housing investment. Congress passed the Act in 1977 to reduce redlining, a practice that discriminates low-income neighborhoods from appropriate lending procedures. While the CRA is noted to have increased the flow of mortgages, with almost $500 billion impacting low- and middle-income communities between 1993 and 1998,[155] recent criticism suggests that the CRA makes the production of low-income housing heavily dependent on banking economics and regulation and not on housing demand. Reclassifying the kinds of investments that qualify under the CRA could result in more efficient and targeted progress, and expanding the CRA to more financial institutions could result in increased investment.

Additionally, on the supply side, suburban neighborhood codes should be updated to remove both implicit and explicit attempts to restrict affordable housing and smaller homes. Local suburban politics can favor the restriction of land supply for rental and affordable housing as well as smaller homes in speculation against neighborhood devaluation. Such policy restricts housing development in high-opportunity neighborhoods, limiting choices for low-income households. Corrective measures would include federal and state governments limiting land and plot-size restrictions and encouraging transparent building codes.

People are focused on what happened 10 years ago [but] we what we really need to focus on is what do we want the housing finance system to look like 10 years or 20 years from now?

—Timothy Mayopoulos, CEO of Fannie Mae, 2012-present[156]

CONCLUSION

The factors behind Fannie's involvement in the Great Recession and 2008 mortgage crisis were not spontaneous, undetectable, or unforeseen. Fannie's history serves as an excellent blueprint to understand how a few critical moments played a role in bringing about a massive financial meltdown. Specifically, conflicting housing policy ideologies and weak business model regulation brought down Fannie Mae. From its beginnings in the New Deal to its botched privatization, and from its expanding business model to its HUD rivalry, Fannie slowly succumbed to its own complexity.

Along the time line of conflicting policy ideologies, Fannie Mae's creation in 1938 suggested that President Roosevelt resorted to the government to create an institution he viewed should ideally be private in nature. Fannie's privatization marked the creation of a weird hybrid between public and private interests, sowing seeds of conflict that have grown throughout Fannie's existence. Although Fannie initially struggled to accept HUD goals and mandates, it soon began manipulating HUD measures: its push to support lower-income housing served to establish a powerful lobbying base.

Soon, the conflict led to weak business model oversight. Stemming from its government-sponsorship status and numerous other advantages established in its 1968 privatization, Fannie grew exponentially. Its ill-regulated development of a guaranty arm in 1981 and the popularization of MBSs through FHEFSSA legislation loopholes in 1992 further contributed to billion-dollar profits. The combination of conflicting public/private interests and unrestrained business model growth ultimately translated into Fannie's purchases of fatally flawed PLS bond and guaranty arm losses, leading to its downfall in the Great Recession.

Despite the decade since Fannie Mae's demise, Fannie's past offers us valuable recommendations in American housing policy for active housing reform. Fannie Mae has been historically regulated passively but never preemptively, from Johnson's privatization in response to Vietnam War debts to Bush's conservatorship in response to the financial crisis, but it is necessary for meaningful *active* reform. Currently, with a passive HUD and strong housing market, the time is right for such rebuilding and improvement. Despite the current political climate, all Americans expect and deserve strong leadership from the White House and Congress. Furthermore, beyond moral and ethical obligations to reform Fannie and Freddie, 2018 marked the first time Fannie and Freddie met their "10% Moment" from original US Treasury and FHFA guidelines, meaning both were able to constitute a 10% annual yield on their preferred stock while also retiring their principal loan values.[157] That makes 2019 an opportune time for reform.

Mortgage Meltdown's twofold proposal of reducing Fannie Mae's liability on taxpayers and supporting homeownership measures offers a comprehensive solution to preempt future mortgage crises while supporting millions of Americans. Fannie's liability is reduced through (a) an eventual reduction in its footprint and size and (b) the introduction of Private Servicer Enterprises (PSEs) into the mortgage market. The PSEs, thoughtfully regulated but independent organizations, would provide a deferring payment mechanism to prevent immediate capital drain, limiting the volatility of the mortgage market, providing stability to all MBS holders, and indirectly supporting the entire American economy. Fannie remains under government conservatorship since its $116 billion taxpayer-funded bailout in 2008, but it continues to play an integral role in housing finance and the housing industry. The risks of rampant homeowner foreclosure can have considerable ramifications on the $25.4 trillion US housing industry, the $10.5 trillion mortgage sector, and the overall economy.[158] A quick escalation in delinquency rates translates into tremendous loss for Fannie and Freddie—up to $100 billion the FHFA estimated in 2017—and without a modified payment policy, taxpayers would ultimately be held liable. In addition to reducing Fannie's liability, systemic risk in the greater financial market would be reduced, response time to crises would be increased, and homeownership would be supported. The concept of payment collaboration between Fannie Mae and the struggling homeowner would not only avert short-term foreclosure but also keep neighborhood home prices stable and add to the intrinsic institutional value of homeownership.

The proposal also details additional methods of supporting homeownership that rely less on Fannie Mae by investigating more direct supply-and-demand measures. Eliminating mortgage lending discrimination and providing greater housing and mortgage access should be priorities in pursuing American homeownership. First-time minority homebuyers can potentially contribute to 75% of America's housing growth over the next decade, and thus methods to restrict discriminatory mortgage lending and improve mortgage access must be explored and supported.[159] Additionally, a steady decline in the homeownership rate from the peak of 69% in the mid-2000s to below 64% in 2017 builds concern about the future of the mortgage and housing sectors. With a current total of 117 million households, an estimated 11 million new households by 2020, and an additional 9 million expected by 2030, America's 134 million in housing stock needs to be expanded.[160]

Fannie Mae presents a fascinating tale but serves as cautionary reminder of what can happen when politics and profits intersect. Fannie's reach has extended far beyond the mortgage market, and it has shaped America, albeit quietly at times, politically, economically, and socially. The far-reaching implications of Fannie Mae have stretched into congressional halls and lobbying campaigns as well as the streets of urban neighborhoods. They've spread deeply into the financial realm, connecting banks, funds, and other financial institutions, while simultaneously straddling HUD goals and regulatory mandates. Yet millions of American homeowners are the real backbone supporting Fannie and Freddie, so we must ensure that the endeavors of these institutions ultimately benefit the very people on which they are dependent.

The difficulty lies, not in the new ideas, but in escaping from the old ones.

—John Maynard Keynes, The General Theory of Employment, Interest, and Money[161]

LIST OF ABBREVIATIONS

FHA *Federal Housing Administration*

Developed in 1934, the FHA was the first government agency to insure mortgage loans; Fannie Mae was later born from this agency.

FHEFSSA *Federal Housing Enterprises Financial Safety and Soundness Act*

A 1992 law that created a new regulator (OFHEO) for Fannie and Freddie.

FHFA *Federal Housing Finance Agency*

The FHFA, created in 2008, took Fannie Mae and Freddie Mac under government conservatorship and still remains as their current regulator.

FHLMC *Federal Home Loan Mortgage Corporation (Freddie Mac)*

FNMA *Federal National Mortgage Association (Fannie Mae)*

G-Fee *Guaranty fee*

The amount charged by Fannie Mae to guarantee mortgages.

GNMA *Government National Mortgage Association (Ginnie Mae)*

A wholly owned government organization (a smaller, all-government-owned sister of Fannie Mae).

GSE *Government-sponsored enterprise*

A congressionally created financial services corporation that supports government initiatives (examples include Fannie, Freddie, and Ginnie).

HARP *Home Affordable Refinance Program*

A federal program to help homeowners who saw a drop in home value refinance with better mortgage terms.

HELOC *Home equity line of credit*

A loan in which a homeowner takes money out of his or her house, essentially using the house as an ATM.

HUD *Department of Housing and Urban Development*

The government agency that generally oversees home mortgage lending practices for underserved and impoverished Americans.

LTV *Loan-to-value*

A financial term used by lenders to express the ratio of a mortgage loan to the home value.

MBS *Mortgage-backed security*

A traded financial instrument (bond) backed by a collection of mortgages.

OFHEO *Office of Federal Housing Enterprise Oversight*

Created in 1992, OFHEO was Fannie and Freddie’s weak regulator.

PLS *Private-label securitization*

The process of creating nongovernment-guaranteed MBS bonds.

NOTES

[1] Hagerty, James R. The Fateful History of Fannie Mae: New Deal Birth to Mortgage Crisis Fall (Charleston, SC: History Press, 2012), 23.

[2] NAHB Staff. "Housing's Contribution to Gross Domestic Product (GDP)." National Association of Homebuilders. (Autumn 2017). www.nahb.org/en/research/housing-economics/housings-economic-impact/housings-contribution-to-gross-domestic-product-gdp.aspx.

[3] Federal National Mortgage Association. *2016 Annual Report Form 10-K.* Washington DC: United States Securities and Exchange Commission. February 17, 2017.

[4] Keynes, John Maynard. "Preface," in *The General Theory of Employment, Interest, and Money* (Cambridge: Cambridge University Press, 1936), 16–18.

[5] Acharya, Viral, Matthew Richardson, Stijin Van Nieuwerburgh, and Lawrence J. White. *Guaranteed to Fail: Fannie Mae, Freddie Mac, and the Debacle of Mortgage Finance* (Princeton, NJ: Princeton University Press, 2011), 20.

[6] Strochack, Sarah, Laurie Goodman, Alanna McCargo, Edward Golding, Jim Parrott, Sheryl Pardo, Todd Hill, Jun Zhu, Bing Bai, Karan Kaul, Bhargavi Ganesh, and Andrea Reyes. *Housing Finance at a Glance: A Monthly Chartbook, December 2017.* Report. December 19, 2017. www.urban.org/research/publication/housing-finance-glance-monthly-chartbook-december-2017.

[7] Defaulting on a mortgage loan can occur through two methods: for a sustained period of time, the homeowner either (a) does not pay the mortgage on time or (b) pays less than the amount that is due. Homeowner delinquency, default, and foreclosure are examined in a following subsection.

[8] Acharya et al., *Guaranteed to Fail*, 9.

[9] Fabozzi, Frank J., Anand K. Bhattacharya, and S. Esther Chang. "Overview of the Mortgage Market," in *The Handbook of Mortgage-Backed Securities*, 5th ed. (Oxford: Oxford University Press, 2001), 4–23.

[10] An escrow arrangement either (a) requires a third party to distribute money between the primary transacting parties or (b) creates a trust account for the borrower to ensure due payment of obligations.

[11] Fabozzi et al., "Overview of the Mortgage Market," 36.

[12] Robertson, Colin. "Mortgage Rate Charts from the Early 1900s." Mortgage and Finances. May 30, 2017. mortgageandfinances.com/check-out-these-mortgage-rate-charts-from-the-early-1900s.

[13] Fabozzi et al., "Overview of the Mortgage Market," 4–23.

[14] Wells Fargo. Wells Fargo & Company Annual Report (2016). Report. January 13, 2017. www08.wellsfargomedia.com/assets/pdf/about/investor-relations/annual-reports/2016-annual-report.pdf.

[15] Securities are tradable financial assets that are bought and sold between investors for investment purposes, and mortgage-backed securities are specifically secured by either residential or commercial mortgages.

[16] Goodman, Laurie, Rolf Pendall, and Jun Zhu. "Headship and Homeownership: What Does the Future Hold?" Urban Institute. June 8, 2015. www.urban.org/research/publication/headship-and-homeownership-what-does-future-hold.

[17] David, Audley. "MBS Primer." John Hopkins Applied Math and Sciences. June 2006. www.ams.jhu.edu/~daudley/448/jhuonly/JPM%20MBS%20Primer.pdf.

[18] Strochack, Sarah, Laurie Goodman, Alanna McCargo, Edward Golding, Jim Parrott, Sheryl Pardo, Todd Hill, Jun Zhu, Bing Bai, Karan Kaul, Bhargavi Ganesh, and Andrea Reyes. *Housing Finance at a Glance: A Monthly Chartbook, December 2017.*

[19] Fannie Mae. "Servicing Guide." Fannie Mae. December 13, 2017. www.fanniemae.com/content/guide/servicing/f/2/09.html.

[20] Not all banks and financial institutions engage in the secondary mortgage market. Some companies, like Quicken Loans, have limited activity in the secondary mortgage market. Other companies both hold a portion of their mortgages as part of their balance sheet and invest a portion in the secondary market.

[21] "Foreclosure Process." US Department of Housing and Urban Development. Accessed January 1, 2018. www.hud.gov/topics/avoiding_foreclosure/foreclosureprocess.

[22] "Foreclosure Process."

[23] "Foreclosure Process."

[24] Boesel, Molly. "Foreclosure Report Highlights: 10-Year Retrospect of the US Residential Foreclosure Crisis." CoreLogic. March 14, 2017. www.corelogic.com/blog/authors/molly-boesel/2017/03/foreclosure-report-highlights-10-year-retrospect-of-the-us-residential-foreclosure-crisis.aspx#.WoIJ_zZU3gV.

[25] Light, Joe. "Fannie-Freddie Might Need $100 billion in New Crisis, FHFA Says." *Bloomberg Business Week*. August 07, 2017. www.bloomberg.com/news/articles/2017-08-07/fannie-freddie-might-need-100-billion-in-new-crisis-fhfa-says.

[26] McLean, Bethany. *Shaky Ground: The Strange Saga of the U.S. Mortgage Giants* (New York, NY: Columbia Global Reports, 2015).

[27] Gilder Lehrman Institute of American History. "Statistics: The American Economy during the 1920s." Gilder Lehrman Institute of American History. Accessed December 17, 2017. www.gilderlehrman.org/content/statistics-american-economy-during-1920s.

[28] USHistory.org Staff. "A Consumer Economy." US History. Accessed December 26, 2017. www.ushistory.org/us/46f.asp.

[29] White, Eugene N., Kenneth Snowden, and Price Fishback, eds. "Lessons from the Great American Real Estate Boom and Bust of the 1920s," in *Housing and Mortgage Markets in Historical Perspective* (Chicago: University of Chicago Press, 2014), 115–24. www.nber.org/chapters/c12797.pdf.

[30] USHistory.org Staff. "The Great Depression." US History. Accessed December 26, 2017. www.ushistory.org/us/48.asp

[31] Hyman, Louis. *Borrow: The American Way of Debt* (New York, NY: Vintage Books Random House, 2012), 60–94.

[32] Hagerty, Fateful History of Fannie Mae, 18–22.

[33] Hyman, *Borrow*, 60–94.

[34] Walters, John R., "Depression-Era Bank Failures: The Great Contagion or the Great Shakeout?" *Economic Quarterly* 91 (2005). www.unc.edu/~salemi/Econ423/Depression_Era_Bank_Failures.pdf.

[35] H.R. Res. 9620, 73 Cong., Congressional Record (1934) (enacted). fraser.stlouisfed.org/files/docs/historical/martin/54_01_19340627.pdf.

[36] Hagerty, Fateful History of Fannie Mae, 22.

[37] Hagerty, Fateful History of Fannie Mae, 23.

[38] Hagerty, Fateful History of Fannie Mae, 24.

[39] Robertson, "Mortgage Rate Charts from the Early 1900s."

[40] Smith, Adam. "An Inquiry into the Nature and Causes of the Wealth of Nations." Library of Economics and Liberty. Accessed December 16, 2017. www.econlib.org/library/Smith/smWN.html.

[41] Hagerty, Fateful History of Fannie Mae, 25.

[42] Hagerty, Fateful History of Fannie Mae, 25.

[43] Hagerty, 30.

[44] Hagerty, 30–32.

[45] Hagerty, 18.

[46] Hagerty, 18.

[47] Hagerty, 18.

[48] Hagerty, 18.

[49] The Government National Mortgage Association (Ginnie Mae) and the Federal Home Loan Mortgage Corporation (Freddie Mac) were established in 1968 and 1970, respectively. Essentially, Ginnie and Freddie were sibling organizations, never growing as large or powerful as Fannie. Although similarities exist between the three, this book explores only Fannie, as generalizing for all three would be inaccurate and unjust.

[50] Hagerty, 37–41.

[51] Acharya et al., *Guaranteed to Fail*, 17.

[52] Federal National Mortgage Association. (2008). *2008 Annual Report Form 10-K.* Washington DC: United States Securities and Exchange Commission. February 27, 2009.

[53] Hagerty, Fateful History of Fannie Mae, 37–41.

[54] Hagerty, 37–41.

[55] Federal National Mortgage Association Charter Act. Title III of the National Housing Act, 12 U.S.C. 1716 et seq., §§ 301-310 (1968). Amended through July 21, 2010. www.fanniemae.com/resources/file/aboutus/pdf/fm-amended-charter.pdf.

[56] H.R. Res. 5334, 102 Cong., Congressional Record (1992) (enacted). www.congress.gov/bill/102nd-congress/house-bill/5334.

[57] Hagerty, Fateful History of Fannie Mae, 139–64.

[58] Weicher, John C. The Affordable Housing Goals, Homeownership and Risk: Some Lessons from Past Efforts to Regulate the GSEs. Report. November 17, 2010. files.stlouisfed.org/files/htdocs/conferences/gse/Weicher.pdf.

[59] *Fannie Mae Historical Conventional Loan Limits*. PDF. Washington DC: Fannie Mae, December 31, 2011. www.fanniemae.com/content/fact_sheet/historical-loan-limits.pdf.

[60] Loan-to-value ratios (LTVs) and FICO credit scores serve as mortgage originators' metrics in determining risk. A low credit score and a high LTV indicates higher risk: the borrower does not have a sound borrowing history and is taking out a loan that is a considerable percentage of the home value.

[61] Acharya et al., *Guaranteed to Fail*, 36.

[62] Federal National Mortgage Association. (2001). *2001 Annual Report Form 10-K.* Washington DC: United States Securities and Exchange Commission. December 31, 2001.

[63] Hagerty, Fateful History of Fannie Mae, 152.

[64] Federal National Mortgage Association. (2003). *2003 Annual Report Form 10-K.* Washington DC: United States Securities and Exchange Commission. March 15, 2003.

[65] Javers, Eamon. "Obama to Overhaul Fannie, Freddie." Politico. March 24, 2010. www.politico.com/story/2010/03/obama-to-overhaul-fannie-freddie-034897.

[66] Securities and Exchange Commission. "Office of the Chief Accountant Issues Statement on Fannie Mae Accounting." News release. December 15, 2004. SEC.gov. www.sec.gov/news/press/2004-172.htm.

[67] Tootell, Geoffrey M. B., Lynn Browne, Alicia Munnell, and James McEneaney. *Mortgage Lending in Boston: Interpreting HMDA Data*. 92, no. 7. (1992 Series). Boston: Federal Reserve Bank of Boston, 1992. Working paper.

[68] Tootell et al., Mortgage Lending in Boston.

[69] Testimony of Pattye Green, Senior Business Manager, Fannie Mae, 108th Cong. (May 3, 2004) (testimony of Pattye Green).

[70] Hagerty, Fateful History of Fannie Mae, 133.

[71] Shinn, Annyis, "Fannie Mae Dissolving Grass-Roots Lobbying Network." *Washington Post*, September 16, 2005. www.washingtonpost.com/wp-dyn/content/article/2005/09/15/AR2005091502341.html.

[72] Shinn, "Fannie Mae Dissolving Grass-Roots Lobbying Network."

[73] Hagerty, Fateful History of Fannie Mae, 128.

[74] Hagerty, 129.

[75] Shinn, "Fannie Mae Dissolving Grass-Roots Lobbying Network."

[76] Statement of Franklin D. Raines, Chairman and CEO of Fannie Mae, Before the U.S. House Committee on Financial Services, 107th Cong. (September 25, 2002) (testimony of Franklin Delano Raines).

[77] Hagerty, Fateful History of Fannie Mae, 60.

[78] Unlike during the Great Depression, banks did not have overwhelming fears about losing money on their loans: market conditions had significantly improved.

[79] Acharya et al., *Guaranteed to Fail*, 32.

[80] Hagerty, Fateful History of Fannie Mae, 60.

[81] Stearns, Janet. "The Low-Income Housing Tax Credit: A Poor Solution to the Housing Crisis." *Yale Law & Policy Review* 6 (1988). digitalcommons.law.yale.edu/ylpr/vol6/iss1/11.

[82] Government-sponsored enterprises (GSEs) are congressionally created, financial-services corporations that support government initiatives. For the housing sectors, the GSEs are Fannie and Freddie.

[i] If $100 worth of mortgages was guaranteed, Fannie Mae needed to have $0.45 in available capital.

[j] If $100 worth of mortgages was held, Fannie needed to have at least $2.50 in available capital.

[83] Acharya et al., *Guaranteed to Fail*, 23–24.

[84] Acharya et al., 23–24.

[85] Hagerty, Fateful History of Fannie Mae, 75.

[86] US Mortgage Securities Issuance. June 21, 2017. Raw data. The Securities Industry and Financial Markets Association, Washington DC.

[87] Frame, W. Scott, Andreas Fuster, Joseph Tracy, and James Vickery. *The Rescue of Fannie Mae and Freddie Mac*. Staff Report #719 (March 2015). United States. Federal Reserve Bank of New York. www.newyorkfed.org/research/staff_reports/sr719.pdf.

[88] US Bond Market Issuance and Outstanding. January 5, 2018. Raw data. The Securities Industry and Financial Markets Association, Washington DC. www.sifma.org/resources/research/us-bond-market-issuance-and-outstanding

[89] Hagerty, James R. "Worst Performer: Countrywide Financial." *Wall Street Journal*, February 25, 2008. www.wsj.com/articles/SB120371017486586357.

[90] Fannie Mae can guarantee loans up to the "conforming" level; a loan value limit of $333,700 and a FICO credit score around 620 were necessities in 2004. The conforming limit adjusts yearly. The current limit is $453,100.

[91] Mortgage refinancing is a process by which homeowners can switch from one teaser rate to another to extend lower short-term rates but it is ultimately an implausible long-term solution.

[92] Hagerty, "Worst Performer," 48.

[93] Hagerty, 48.

[94] US Mortgage Securities Issuance. June 21, 2017. Raw data. The Securities Industry and Financial Markets Association, Washington DC. www.sifma.org/wp-content/uploads/2017/06/sf-us-mortgage-related-sifma.xls

[95] Tranching is a process of splitting up mortgage bonds by risk assessment to give suitable terms to specific investors. Each tranche, or slice, is representative of a different level of risk.

[96] Nieuwerburgh, Stijin Van. *Guaranteed to Fail: Lunch Talk at NYU*. (Transcription of talk given at New York University's Stern School of Business, November 1, 2011). people.stern.nyu.edu/svnieuwe/GTF_Stern_November12011.pdf

[97] Nieuwerburgh, Guaranteed to Fail: Lunch Talk at NYU.

[98] The Securities Industry and Financial Markets Association (SIFMA). "How Do Credit Ratings Affect Yield?" Investing in Bonds. Accessed December 01, 2017. www.investinginbonds.com/learnmore.asp?catid=5&subcatid=19&id=190.

[99] Mattingly, Phil. "Justice Department Says Evidence Shows S&P Inflated Bond Ratings." *Bloomberg BusinessWeek*. March 16, 2013. www.bloomberg.com/news/articles/2013-03-06/evidence-shows-s-p-inflated-bond-ratings-holder-says.

[100] Gopal, Prashant. "U.S. Homeownership Rate Falls to the Lowest Since 1995." *Bloomberg Business Week*. April 29, 2014. www.bloomberg.com/news/articles/2014-04-29/u-s-homeownership-rate-falls-to-the-lowest-since-1995

[101] Gopal, "U.S. Homeownership Rate Falls."

[102] Nieuwerburgh, Guaranteed to Fail: Lunch Talk at NYU.

[103] Acharya et al., Guaranteed to Fail, 47.

[104] Nieuwerburgh, Guaranteed to Fail: Lunch Talk at NYU.

[105] McLean, *Shaky Ground*, 91–101.

[106] Federal National Mortgage Association. (2008). *2008 Annual Report Form 10-K.*

[107] Acharya et al., Guaranteed to Fail, 47.

[108] Duhigg, Charles. "Doubts Raised on Big Backers of Mortgages." *New York Times*, May 05, 2008. www.nytimes.com/2008/05/06/business/06fannie.html.

[109] Loan accessibility is measured by falling LTV ratios, stricter FICO score requirements, and falling debt-to-income ratios of borrowers. The overall tightening of these lending parameters is referred to as a "credit crunch."

[110] Dayen, David. "African-Americans Are Still Being Victimized by the Mortgage Market." New Republic. May 27, 2014. newrepublic.com/article/117912/reparations-how-mortgage-market-hurts-african-americans.

[111] Goodman, Laurie, Jun Zhu, and Taz George. "Where Have All the Loans Gone? The Impact of Credit Availability on Mortgage Volume." Urban Institute. March 13, 2014. www.urban.org/research/publication/where-have-all-loans-gone-impact-credit-availability-mortgage-volume.

[112] McLean, Shaky Ground, 35.

[113] Federal National Mortgage Association. (2007). *2007 Annual Report Form 10-K.* Washington DC: United States Securities and Exchange Commission. February 27, 2008.

[114] Hagerty, Fateful History of Fannie Mae, 144–86.

[115] Explaining the Great Recession in so few pages would be an injustice to its complexity. This book examines only Fannie Mae's involvement with a few other institutions (like rating agencies and PLS originators). In reality, many banks, originators, rating agencies, regulators, and other institutions were involved in bringing about the Great Recession. Collectively, systemic risk, or the risk of the system as a whole, was the ultimate factor.

[116] McLean, *Shaky Ground,* 34–44.

[117] McLean, *Shaky Ground,* 34–44.

[118] Acharya et al., *Guaranteed to Fail*, 75–76.

[119] Acharya et al., *Guaranteed to Fail,* 90–91.

[120] Acharya et al., *Guaranteed to Fail*, 61–79.

[121] Glassman, James, and Alex Pollock. "How to Fix Fannie and Freddie." Politico. March 1, 2016. www.politico.com/agenda/story/2016/1/how-to-fix-fannie-and-freddie-000027.

[122] McLean, Shaky Ground, 40

[123] Light, Joe. "Fannie-Freddie Keep Giving Profits to U.S. Amid Talks on Changes." *Bloomberg Business Week*. September 29, 2017. www.bloomberg.com/news/articles/2017-09-29/fannie-freddie-keep-giving-profits-to-u-s-amid-talks-on-changes.

[124] McLean, Shaky Ground, 44.

[125] Sorkin, Andrew. Too Big to Fail: The Inside Story of How Wall Street and Washington Fought to Save the Financial System—and Themselves. (New York, NY: Viking Press, 2009)

[126] Refinancing is a process that gives homeowners access to a new mortgage loan that replaces the existing one. The new loan features a customizable mortgage rate, loan length, and principal. Refinances can be used to reduce a homeowner's monthly mortgage payment.

[127] Cohen, Betsalel. "The Boxer-Menendez Refinance Bill-HARP 2.5?" Bills. March 11, 2013. www.bills.com/boxer-menendez-and-harp-2-mortgage.

[128] McLean, *Shaky Ground,* 100–101.

[129] "Congress Considers GSE G-Fee Increase to Pay for Tax Cut Extensions." NCSHA.org. December 16, 2011. www.ncsha.org/blog/congress-considers-gse-g-fee-increase-pay-tax-cut-extensions.

[130] McLean, *Shaky Ground,* 131–34.

[131] Shenn, Jody. "Fannie Mae to Pay Treasury $59.4 billion after Record Profit." *Bloomberg Business Week.* May 9, 2013. www.bloomberg.com/news/articles/2013-05-09/fannie-mae-to-pay-treasury-59-4-billion-after-record-profit-1-

[132] Light, Joe. "Bonds Shift Risk from Taxpayers." *Wall Street Journal*, December 30, 2015, Money & Investing sec.

[133] Fannie Mae. "Credit Risk Sharing." Fannie Mae. December 13, 2017. www.fanniemae.com/portal/funding-the-market/credit-risk/index.html.

[134] Classick, Matthew. "Fannie Mae Prices $1.494 billion Connecticut Avenue Securities Risk Sharing Deal." Fannie Mae. February 6, 2018. www.fanniemae.com/portal/media/financial-news/2018/connecticut-avenue-securities-2018-01-6664.html.

[135] Strochack et al., Housing Finance at a Glance: A Monthly Chartbook, December 2017.

[136] Cole, Wendy. "Bethany McLean: Exposing the Fig Leaf." March 2011. peterkellerpc.blogspot.com.

[137] Strochack et al., Housing Finance at a Glance.

[138] Strochack et al., Housing Finance at a Glance.

[139] Strochack et al., Housing Finance at a Glance.

[140] From this subsection onward, the proposal is pertinent to both Fannie and Freddie (both GSEs).

[141] Fannie Mae. "Servicing Guide." Fannie Mae. December 13, 2017. www.fanniemae.com/content/guide/servicing/f/2/09.html.

[142] Strochack et al., Housing Finance at a Glance.

[143] Strochack et al., Housing Finance at a Glance.

[144] This test included provisions for a 6.5% decline in GDP, a rise in the unemployment rate to 10%, and a 25% fall in home prices.

[145] Light, Joe. "Fannie-Freddie Might Need $100 billion in New Crisis, FHFA Says." *Bloomberg Business Week*. August 07, 2017. www.bloomberg.com/news/articles/2017-08-07/fannie-freddie-might-need-100-billion-in-new-crisis-fhfa-says.

[146] Bakel, Pete. "Fannie Mae Reports Net Income of $3.2 billion and Comprehensive Income of $3.1 billion for Q2 2017." Fannie Mae. August 3, 2017. www.fanniemae.com/portal/media/financial-news/2017/second-quarter-2017-financial-results-6585.html.

[147] Brennan, Maya, Pamela Blumenthal, Laurie Goodman, Ellen Seidman, and Brady Meixell. "Housing as an Asset Class." Urban Institute. October 02, 2017. www.urban.org/research/publication/housing-asset-class.

[148] Andriotis, Anna Maria, and Rachel Louise Ensign. "Hudson City Settles Discriminatory-Lending Allegations for About $33 million." *Wall Street Journal*, September 24, 2015. www.wsj.com/articles/hudson-city-settles-discriminatory-lending-charges-for-about-33-million-1443112730.

[149] Lane, Ben. "BancorpSouth Fined $10.6 million for Discriminatory Lending, Redlining." Housing Wire. June 29, 2016. www.housingwire.com/articles/37405-bancorpsouth-fined-106-million-for-discriminatory-lending-redlining.

[150] Goodman, Laurie, Alanna McCargo, Edward Golding, Bing Bai, Bhargavi Ganesh, and Sarah Strochak. "Barriers to Accessing Homeownership." Urban Institute. November 16, 2017. Accessed February 12, 2018. www.urban.org/research/publication/barriers-accessing-homeownership.

[151] "Cost burdened" refers to families that spend 30% or more of their income on housing needs.

[152] Brennan et al., "Housing as an Asset Class."

[153] "The State of the Nation's Housing 2017." Joint Center for Housing Studies, Harvard University. June 16, 2017. www.jchs.harvard.edu/research/state_nations_housing.

[154] Goodman et al., "Barriers to Accessing Homeownership."

[155] Litan, Robert E., Retsinas, Nicolas P., Belsky, Eric S., Haag, and Susan White. "The Community Reinvestment Act After Financial Modernization: A Baseline Report" (PDF). US Department of the Treasury. April 19, 2000, 16–17.

[156] Ryssdal, Kai, and Bridget Bodnar. "Fannie Mae CEO Reflects on Housing 10 years After the Financial Crisis." Marketplace. January 24, 2018. www.marketplace.org/2018/01/24/business/corner-office-divided-decade/fannie-mae-ceo-reflects-housing-10-years-after.

[157] Glassman and Pollock, "How to Fix Fannie and Freddie."

[158] Strochack et al., Housing Finance at a Glance.

[159] "The State of the Nation's Housing 2017." Joint Center for Housing Studies, Harvard University.

[160] Brennan et al., "Housing as an Asset Class."

[161] Keynes, "Preface," 16–18.

Note: This book discusses Fannie Mae and not Freddie Mac or Ginnie Mae, Fannie's sibling organizations. The "Recommendations" section, however, is pertinent to both Fannie and Freddie (government-sponsored agencies) but not Ginnie (a fully government-owned enterprise).

www.ingramcontent.com/pod-product-compliance
Lightning Source LLC
LaVergne TN
LVHW022314200926
848481LV00004B/1340
9781807650551